Joseph Ferguson

Life-Struggles in Rebel Prisons

A Record of the Sufferings, Escapes, Adventures and Starvation of the Union Prisoners

Joseph Ferguson

Life-Struggles in Rebel Prisons
A Record of the Sufferings, Escapes, Adventures and Starvation of the Union Prisoners

ISBN/EAN: 9783337125738

Printed in Europe, USA, Canada, Australia, Japan

Cover: Foto ©ninafisch / pixelio.de

More available books at **www.hansebooks.com**

Truly Yours,
Joseph Ferguson

LIFE-STRUGGLES

IN

REBEL PRISONS:

A RECORD OF

The Sufferings, Escapes, Adventures and Starvation
of the Union Prisoners.

BY JOSEPH FERGUSON,

Late Captain First New Jersey Vols.

CONTAINING AN APPENDIX WITH THE NAMES, REGIMENTS, AND
DATE OF DEATH OF PENNSYLVANIA SOLDIERS
WHO DIED AT ANDERSONVILLE.

WITH AN INTRODUCTION BY REV. JOSEPH T. COOPER, D. D.

"Wherein I spake of most disastrous chances,
Of moving accidents by flood and field,
Of hair-breadth scapes i' th' imminent deadly breach;
Of being taken by the insolent foe,
And sold to slavery; of my redemption thence,
And with it all my travel's history."

PHILADELPHIA, PA.,
JAMES M. FERGUSON, PUBLISHER,
No. 25 North Sixth Street.
1865.

Entered according to Act of Congress, in the Year 1865, by

JOSEPH FERGUSON,

In the Office of the Clerk of the District Court for the Eastern District of Pennsylvania.

GEO. S. FERGUSON, PR., 25 N. 6TH ST.   ILLUSTRATED BY VAN INGEN & SNYDER.

THIS BOOK IS DEDICATED TO

My Mother,

WHO FIRST TAUGHT ME TO ADVOCATE

TRUTH, JUSTICE AND FREEDOM,

AND INSTILLED INTO MY MIND

The Principles of a True Religion.

CONTENTS.

CHAPTER I.

Opening of the Spring Campaign of 1864—Skirmishing—Battles of the Wilderness and Spotsylvania C. H.—General Grant—Death of General Sedgwick—Taken Prisoner—"Come out of that Coat"—The Chivalry, ... 17

CHAPTER II.

No More War—Welcome to Soldiers—Happy Hearts—Home—Justice to Traitors—General Lee—Lee's Body Guard—"Stop Thief"—Confederate Officers—Horrible Place, . . . 25

CHAPTER III.

Libby Prison—Vermin and "Skirmishing"—The Rebel Joke—Belle Isle—The Bloodhound—Rebels Wearing Uncle Sam's Clothing—Hostages—Foote—Castle Thunder—Colonel Streight and his Escape—Plot for the Capture of Richmond—Minstrels—Justice, - 33

CHAPTER IV.

Boy Heroes—Bravery—An Exhibition—Southern Ladies—"Down with the Traitor"—The Drunken Confederate Major—Pickpockets and Thieves—Cheerfulness Necessary to Health,   -   43

CHAPTER V.

Rebel Humanity—Death—Home—Mother—Three Officers Escape—The Fire-eater—Danville—Jeff. Davis—Guards—Water—Food—Hope,   -   -   51

CHAPTER VI.

No Exchange—Rebel Honor—The Southern Paradise—Salisbury and its Horrors—Patriotic Family—Major Gee—Starvation—The Cat—Lieut. Davis Murdered—Vengeance—Charlotte—Columbia—Augusta—Bradford the Black-Leg—Baltimore Thugs,   -   -   -   -   -   -   56

CHAPTER VII.

Escape from the Rebels—Freedom, but Dangers—In the Woods—Plans—Negroes—The Loyal, Christian Slave—Race for Liberty—No Food—Bloodhounds—Recapture—No Mercy—Jail—A Fight with Rats,   -   -   -   -   -   -   63

CHAPTER VIII.

Andersonville and its Butchers—Punishment for its Villainous Keepers—Justice—No Quarters—Food—Wood and Water—The Hounds—Death and Suffering—The Hospital—Testimony—Brutality—No Mercy—God will Punish the Guilty, - - - - - - - - 72

CHAPTER IX.

Macon Military Prison—Stockade—Guards—"Look Out for the Dead Line"—Quarters—Washing—Food—Wood—Water—Rations and Cooking Utensils—Yankee Ingenuity—Sutlering—Insults—The Boys are Coming! - - - - - 88

CHAPTER X.

Preaching—Consolation of Religion—Non-Combatants—The Chaplain and Rebel General—Rebel Officers Stealing—Federal Officer "Bucked"—Rumors—Gambling—"Fresh Fish"—Amusements, 95

CHAPTER XI.

The Georgia Militia—Murder of Lieutenant Gierson—Plans for an Uprising—Spies—Remarkable Escapes—Captain Gibbs—Tunneling—Traitors—4th of July Celebration—Sherman—"Tramp, Tramp"—Lieutenant Davis, - - - - 102

CHAPTER XII.

Savannah Prison—Nearly Recaptured—Incident on Route—A Southern Mother Fooled—Our Parade in Savannah—Secesh Females—Our Quarters—Food and Water—The Sutler—Cow Falls into a Tunnel—A Federal Officer becomes Crazy—Escapes—Hardships, - - - - - 113

CHAPTER XIII.

Southern Feeling—Charleston the Cradle of Rebellion—Under Fire—Jail Yard—No Food or Quarters—Fires—Shelling the City—Barbarity on Colored Soldiers—Convicts—The Cowardly Leader, 123

CHAPTER XIV.

Take a Parole to Live—Power of Attorney—Selfishness—Yellow Fever—Sisters of Charity—Vagabonds—The Silent City—Fires—Escapes—Hardee—A True Lady—Mercy, - - - 132

CHAPTER XV.

Columbia Military Prison—Procuring Meat—Camp Sorghum—Food, Wood and Water—Rebel Atrocity—Lieutenant Parker Torn by Dogs—Escapes—Murder of Lieutenant Turbayne—Special Exchanges—Southern Robbers, - - - 142

CHAPTER XVI.

Insane Asylum Prison—An Ugly Face—Appearance of Prisoners—Food, Wood and Water—No Quarters—Suffering—Sickness—Drunken Doctors—Sutler's Prices—Bill of Exchange—Richland Jail—Incident of the Meal-Sack—The Spy—Dr. Palmer, the Preaching Rebel—"Sherman's March to the Sea," - - - - - - 154

CHAPTER XVII.

"Sherman's Coming"—Excited Rebels—Southern Despotism—The Braggart South Carolinians—The Cadets—A Prison Brings Grey Hairs—The Dead Winder and the Living Wirz—Escapes and Hardships—The Union League—The Poor Union Woman, - - - - - - - - 168

CHAPTER XVIII.

Southern Rail-roads—Accidents—Fresh Beef—Exchange Rumors—"Snuff Dippers"—Murder of Captain Evens—Prison at Charlotte—Story of an Escape—Oath of Allegiance Men—Paroled—Homeward—What a Secessionist thought of a Copperhead—Break Down—Raleigh—Goldsborough—Suffering Union Boys—In Our Own Lines—Joy, - - - - - - 178

CHAPTER XIX.

"Up From the Valley of Death"—The Reception Given to Us—Plenty to Eat and Gladness of Heart—Wilmington—Annapolis—Skeletons Among Their Friends—Altered Appearance of Officers—Honorably Discharged—Home—Let Us Have Justice, - - - - - - 201

APPENDIX.

Names, Regiments and Date of Death of Pennsylvania Soldiers who died at Andersonville.

INTRODUCTION.

Peace reigns once more throughout the land. No longer

> "Doth dogged war bristle his angry crest."

A blessed change has taken place—a change which, when contemplated in contrast with the scenes through which our country has lately been passing, should awaken emotions of gratitude to God in every heart. Yes, as we look back upon the storm that was raging a short time ago in such wild and terrific fury in the land—as we recur to the desolations which it left behind it, it surely becomes us as Christian patriots to recognise in the arrest that has been put upon its career the goodness of Him who "maketh wars to cease unto the end of the earth!" Alas! that there are so many who seem to have but little sense of the value of this precious boon of peace, and of the source from which it has come!

Such narratives of toil and suffering as the one presented by the author of these pages is calculated to impress the heart with a sense of the worth of peace, and of the kindness of God in vouchsafing it to our country.

But while our thanksgivings are, first of all, due to the Supreme Ruler of the Universe, let us not forget our indebtedness to the *soldier* who, prompted by a noble love of country, so freely devoted to its interests everything which he held dear in this world, even to life itself.

A perusal of the pages of this book will, we think, stir the soul of every patriot. He will here see how strong is the claim to our gratitude which those have who so bravely shared the dangers of the battle-field and the horrors of the prison-house. A feeling of this sort ought, one would suppose, to be sufficient to awaken a deep-felt interest in the sad and heart-melting pictures of human suffering, which, from what we know of the character of the author, we cannot doubt are truthful representations. In some instances we shall, no doubt, be disposed to think that, perhaps, the pictures here drawn have received a darker shade of coloring than the reality would justify. Had these representations been made several months ago, we would certainly, although not doubting the sincerity of the author, have felt inclined to think that, perhaps, the truth was too strongly stated. The statements here made, however, not only carry on their face the marks of truth, but are in such perfect harmony with the representations of others, and some of these witnesses speaking under the dread sanction of an oath, that we are compelled to give them our credence.

And what humiliating revelations are here made! How forcibly must these details impress the heart of the Christian with the fact of the fearful depravity of human nature, and the lengths to which it may go in the perpetration of wickedness. This, at least, will be one effect which a perusal of these pages must produce.

Another result, doubtless, will be a higher appreciation of the liberties which we enjoy as a people. Surely, we cannot set too high a value upon blessings for which a price so costly has been paid. Let us not fail, reader, as we turn the leaves of this book to be reminded of the worth of those free institutions which are the the glory of our Republic, and which, at a sacrifice so great, have been rescued from the bloody grasp of slavery.

J. T. C.

LIFE-STRUGGLES

IN

REBEL PRISONS.

CHAPTER I.

Opening of the spring campaign of 1864—Skirmishing—Battles of the Wilderness and Spottsylvania C. H.—General Grant—Death of General Sedgwick—Taken Prisoner—"Come out of that Coat"—The Chivalry.

> "Forever float that standard sheet!
> Where breathes the foe but falls before us,
> With Freedom's soil beneath our feet,
> And Freedom's banner streaming o'er us."

The spring of 1864 opened with every indication that the insurgents in arms would receive such terrible blows from the soldiers of the Union that peace might be expected ere another year had taken its flight. Every loyal heart felt confident that the Government had in itself the power and will, if wisely employed, to crush the monster rebellion. Every true citizen and honest heart possessed faith in the manly boys who had been battling for years, and who, at Gettysburg, proved the Northerner was more than a match for the boastful Southerner. The re-enlisting of the veterans of fifty battles was a pledge of the Union's restoration.

B

Who was better able to judge of the feasibility of putting down the traitors than those who had been in the front rank, in defeat and victory? They said:

> "Freedom's battle once begun,
> Bequeathed by bleeding sire to son,
> Though baffled oft is ever won."

Victories had been proclaimed east and west; the loyal North felt satisfied and rejoiced. The first of May the weather was delightful; the sun shone forth with a brilliancy that displayed the glory of its great Creator The leaden skies of winter had departed, and the light and life of the coming summer dawned on the Potomac Army breaking camp, for another onward march to Richmond. The days of reviews, drills and parades were past; the time had again arrived to "pack up," which meant skirmishes, battles, sufferings and death. The army was never in better spirits. A smile of satisfaction rested on the faces of the soldiers, as they took down their shelter-tents from the winter huts to roll on the knapsack. As the "assembly" sounded on the clear air of a May morning, the soldiers fell promptly into their places, whilst cheer after cheer went up from the soil of the Old Dominion for the Union and the new commander, General Grant, the hero of the Mississippi Valley. The hearts of all were merry as the column wound its way over plain, through wood, and across the famous Rapidan River. General Grant kept up no connection with his old base, Brandy Station, but swung out into the unknown and untried Wildernesses of Virginia, where so many lives had been lost previously. He trusted in God, and the heroic valor of his brave spirits to open a new base. The sequel and career of his army proves that it was not misplaced confidence. The army was put in battle array, and dispositions made for a terrible conflict. Drummer boys and soldiers bearing stretchers were to be seen following closely the advancing regiments. Surgeons were seen establishing field-hospitals, a sure indication that bloody work will take place. Early in the morning the sharp crack of the skirmisher's rifle could be heard, and as the day advanced the reports of the rifles increased, whilst occasionally a wounded man came limping from the front. The ghastly work began in earnest. The enemy's skirmishers fell behind their line of works, and now a fierce musketry and artillery fire announced that the sanguinary battles of the Wilderness had commenced. It was a long time before General Grant discovered the real position of the enemy, owing to the thick growth of scrub oak. On the fifth of May, both parties fought with persistent valor, neither attaining a permanent advantage. This struggle in the forest we believe to be the greatest bushwhacking battle of the war. It was fought at close range; in some parts of the line twelve yards did not interv'ene between the contending armies. The eye could only catch occasional glimpses of the rebels.

At my side a young man was killed, who died easier than any person I have ever seen fall by a bullet. The ball entered his neck, striking an artery; he bled to death in a few seconds. A sigh or a groan never escaped from him; he dropped slowly on his knees as the soul took its flight to God. Another brave boy had a ball pass through both his cheeks, and strange to say his jaw and teeth remained unharmed, not even scratched. It is evident he was yawning or shouting at the time. A tall muscular man had just pulled the trigger of his rifle, when a ball shattered his forehead, scattering his brains over me. Lieut. Swan, as brave a soldier as ever faced a foe and as kind-hearted a gentleman as ever breathed the pure air of heaven, was struck by a cannon-ball and died in great agony. May his memory remain forever green in the hearts of his comrades. Though he suffered much previous to his death, when the time came for the soul's flight, a smile lit up his feminine features that brought tears of joy to the eyes of those present. There was a soldier who had a round shot pass through his breast; a companion stooped to take his watch and a likeness of a dear one at home, when his heart dropped on the ground. Nothing alarmed, the sympathizing friend procured the watch and memento of home, and afterwards forwarded them to his mourning relations.

On the evening of the sixth of May the rebels succeeded in occupying a position on our right, and for half an hour or so had the advantage, owing to a panic among several regiments on the flank. Three gallant soldiers, Colonel William Henry and Captain Roberts, of the Jersey Brigade, and Colonel Higginbotham, of the New York Chasseurs, rallied several hundred men and kept the rebels at bay until a new line was established. The country owes them a debt of gratitude for bravery and foresight on this trying occasion. They prevented a rout in the army. As I have never seen an acknowledgment of their gallantry, I place their names on record as *one* who will do them justice.

The traitors, as usual, fought behind breastworks, and the army of the Union suffered heavily in killed and wounded. There have been few battles of the war showing a greater loss in officers; my Regiment lost fourteen out of eighteen. By repulsing the Government troops the traitors became bolder, and in turn attacked. For a short time they had a temporary success, but were severely chastised for their recklessness. Our boys had hastily constructed a rifle-pit, and the rebels in assaulting were mowed down in hundreds. General Grant formed a new line.

Skirmishing and fighting were carried on during

the seventh of May, the rebels taking the offensive. Had it been any other general but Grant we would have recrossed the Rapidan, and lay inactive during the spring and summer. But General Grant is a man who will not go backward if he cannot go forward. The army now made a movement to Spottsylvania Court House. At this place there were sanguinary combats, and here were made the most desperate charges and counter-charges of the war. Major General Sedgwick was killed not twenty yards from where I stood. The "grey-jackets" got the worst of it in all these bloody battles. In one charge the Second Corps took 7,000 prisoners and 20 pieces of cannon.

The circumstances under which officers and men are taken prisoners are as varied as possible. None are captured at the rear; occasionally a straggler is picked up by guerillas. It is generally in the front rank, struggling manfully, the soldier falls into the hands of the enemy. He soon learns he is in the hands of the rebels by a brutal order to "Come out of those boots;" "I want your watch and money;" "I'll trade hats;" "Give me your knife and pocketbook;" "You 'uns dress well." A man is fortunate who gets into prison with a respectable dress, money, or anything valuable. But I will tell, you before I proceed with this volume, how I fell into the hands of the chivalry.

On the morning of the twelfth of May my regiment was ordered to advance, assault and drive the rebels from a strong breastwork. We pushed boldly forward, but when two hundred yards from the rebel line, encountered a withering fire of grape and canister, musketry, etc., besides felled trees, *abattis*, and every species of obstacle calculated to retard our passage. My soldier companions fell in scores. I commanded a company of as gallant boys as ever fired a gun, who never feared the foe wherever found. We crossed the network barring our passage, and clambered over the breastworks. Some of the rebels who refused to surrender, were bayoneted, their comrades fleeing. Our support failed to come up, and the rebels being reinforced, they returned to the encounter. Our boys fought with heroism for the possession of the works, but only to fall in the good cause. The rebels made a charge on our right, and in a moment were in our rear. I soon comprehended we were surrounded, and I would be taken prisoner,—what I most dreaded in all my soldier life. Frightful thought! During the excitement I voluntarily uttered a prayer I learned in childhood at my mother's knees. As my lips ceased to move, a ball struck me on the neck, abrading the skin, and causing a small flow of blood, when I was called upon to surrender; but the scoundrels did not cease firing at me. Another ball passed through my coat. O, the unmerciful cut-throats! For an instant the rebels surrounding us were forced back, and in the confusion I made an attempt to escape, by jumping in a small gulley and laying flat, in the centre of a pile of Union and rebel dead. I now lay between both lines of battle, and for the space of half an hour the conflict raged. During this time I must have been out of my mind, for I never experienced greater mental suffering. The dead around me formed a breast-work. There was a rain-storm at the time, but the drops from the sky did not seem to fall faster or closer than the murderous missiles of the contestants. I lay one hundred and fifty yards from our line of battle, and about twenty-five from the rebels. To have gone into either would have been certain death. Each party held their ground. The struggle was over. I impatiently awaited the advance of either party to release me from what was worse than death—the agony of suspense. In a few minutes the rebel skirmishers stealthily crept out to where I lay, and as I did not move, they took me to be dead. I raised my body slightly, and as I did so, a rebel ruffian, with an oath, told me to get to the rear. In a shorter time than I can tell now, I was on my way to General Lee's headquarters, under guard of as ragged and hard-looking a man as ever fought in Jeff.'s and Satan's cause. Now commenced one of the greatest year's sufferings that it has ever been my lot to undergo.

CHAPTER II.

No More War—Welcome to Soldiers—Happy Hearts—Home—Justice to Traitors—General Lee—Lee's Body Guard—"Stop Thief"—Confederate Officers—Horrible Place.

> "Columbia, Columbia! to glory arise,
> The queen of the world, and the child of the skies!"

What a balm to the hearts of those who love their country that the war is over! Peace again smiles upon our land. The mustering, marshalling, marching, sieging and battling, are events of the past. Mothers and sisters, fathers and brothers are every day welcoming the gallant braves of the the Union army, as they return to their homes, throwing aside the weapons of death to resume the pursuits of peace—to live quietly as citizens of the country they saved—to help on the glory and prosperity of the great American nation. They return conscious of having discharged their duty, and released four millions of their fellow-beings from bondage. Happy must be their hearts in the thought that their bayonets and bullets knocked off the fetters of so many of their black-skinned countrymen, and made their country free in fact as well as name. It did my heart good to see the welcome these noble boys received in Washington, as they marched with proud step and manly bearing by their President, their torn and tattered flags giving evidence of the terrible scenes of carnage they had passed through.

Alas! readers, how many thousands of the nation's sons will never return! They cemented with their blood devotion to right, justice, truth and sound principle. "They sleep their last sleep, they have fought their last battle." The soldiers of the United States have on all the battle-fields of the insurrection displayed a Christian magnanimity towards the blood-thirsty men of the South. The guards on southern prisons stood with loaded rifles, cocked, ready to kill an unarmed captive, even inside the prescribed prison bounds, that a furlough might be procured. This, or a corporal's stripes, was the price paid for outrage and murder. The men who died by inches, for want of care and food, at Libby, Columbia, Savannah, Florence and Andersonville, and all the southern hells, showed their faith in the government for which they went forth to battle. Coercion never won them over to the Devil's cause of a Southern Confederacy. Punishment, threats, the want of food, never seduced their allegiance from the old flag. In the same death-sentence calling for bread, God's blessing was implored on the country. A prayer was offered at the throne of grace for the nation's redemption, prosperity and happiness. Some forty-five thousand could, and did, die, but could never prove recreant to the trust reposed in them by Columbia. They had no welcome home from loving, over-joyed hearts, but let us hope there was rejoicing in the paradise of the holy and just; that there was a greeting for them in the abode of bliss, where war, prisons, brutality and disloyalty have no entrance. Noble martyrs! History will cast a light and beam of glory over their sufferings and triumphant death, that will draw the sympathy and admiration of the pure-minded over the whole world.

Jeff. Davis and all his associates are in the government prisons. I desire to see justice administered to them. If it is, they will be hung, or capital punishment should be abolished. An example is needed. I want to see *him* hung, and am careless whether it is on the gallows or a "sour apple tree."

After falling into the hands of the rebels, and whilst being conducted to the rear, an incident took place which may not be uninteresting. A wounded rebel begged my guard and "the writer" to place him under cover from the fire of the Union troops. I have never, in camp or upon the field of battle, resisted the call for mercy, or passed by a suffering soldier, enemy or not, when in my power to alleviate agony. We raised the wounded rebel and were carrying him to a place of safety, when a round shot, from one of our batteries, took off the head of my guard. I carried or rather dragged the afflicted man into a hollow, where there was a small stream of water. He fainted away, and I sat pondering on the exciting scenes through which I had just passed, when an officer, a villain, made his appearance, and in a brutal manner told me to go with him. I had gone but a few steps when he called some soldiers and ordered them to examine my person and relieve me of my effects. Telling me to unbutton my overcoat, he seized my sword-belt rudely, (I had broken my sword, thinking if I could not use it no rebel ever should,) and put it on himself. He took my watch and chain, and all the money I possessed, some forty-dollars. I remonstrated against being thus "shaven and shorn," but only received abuse. A short time afterwards, I was handed over to what I took to be the provost guard, and taken to Lee's head-quarters. I made enquiries for the name of the Southern gentleman who robbed me, but without success. Thanking God I had got out of his hands, and trying to believe that all the rebels were not like him, I plodded through the mud with a light heart. I was now put in a field with several hundred of my Union brethren, and felt rejoiced I was again in company with loyal, honest men. I saw General Lee here. After stopping in the field for two days, and living on four crackers and a supply of water from a muddy brook, we were moved to Gordonsville.

It rained almost the entire journey. The roads were in a dreadful condition, and the poor, hungry Union soldiers dragged themselves through the slush. A large number fell in the mud and water never to rise again. One light-haired boy, with whom I had shared my last cracker, as the pangs of hunger gnawed on his vitals, could go no further and sank in the road, when a cowardly guard struck him with his sabre, and with an oath told him to go on. I moved on with the column; no doubt he is one of the the victims of rebel cruelty, mourned for in a Northern home. We were guarded by a troop of cavalry styling themselves General Lee's Body Guard, but a more dastardly organization of robbers never sat on horses. They watched every opportunity to goad, taunt, steal from and maltreat the unfortunates in their charge. With a Quixotic air they would sneeringly ask us, "Will you take a ride?"

Halting in a field for a night, utterly prostrated with the fatigues of the day, my clothes wet through, and thinking of something to eat, I lay down on the wet earth and was soon asleep. About midnight I felt a pulling at my head and jumped up. One of the guards had seized my felt hat and made off with it. I shouted "Stop thief! Guard, don't let that man pass you; he's got my hat!" as I ran after the grey-back. On reaching the guard line, I was told to go back, as the sentry leveled his carbine at me, whilst the rascal walked leisurely away with my hat. Thus I became hatless, but found some of my fellow-prisoners in other parts of the camp were treated in a similar way. Several had their shoes stolen as they slept. It was a pitiful sight next morning to see us painfully toiling over the disagreeable roads of Virginia hatless and shoeless. The plan to deprive us of the most valuable part of our clothing had been systematically arranged between the guards, to be carried into effect when we halted. A rebel had the hardihood to wear my hat; taking off the gold cord, he was under the impression I would not recognize it. I told the officer about it; he said he would get it for me, but failed to do so.

In many regiments of the rebel army there is a tacit understanding among officers and men for fleecing the "blue bellies," as the rebels style Uncle Sam's soldiers, who may have the misfortune to fall into their power. A Confederate officer sees a felt hat (something scarce in the South) he would like to possess, but has not the honor of a man who would ask for an honest trade, or give a fair remuneration for it, tells one of his men to offer a corn-dodger for it, and if not accepted, to take it, or steal it. A soldier who by strategy got a silver watch into prison, lost it in the following way: The officer of the day had seen it one day at roll-call and sent word to the Yankee he desired to see him at his office under guard.

Rebel—"You've got a watch; what will you take for it."

Prisoner—"I don't want to sell it; but as I can't live on your rations, I'll part with it so I may sustain life."

Rebel—I have'nt got the money at present to buy it; but there is a wealthy gentleman across the way who will give you a good price for it, and if you have confidence in me, I'll show it to him and sell it for you. You'll get the money to-night."

The officer had been sick with dysentery for a time, and to buy strengthening food to prolong life, parted with his timepiece. It, or money, never afterwards came into his possession. The officer and *gentleman* of the Confederate States lied every day in some excuse when the poor captive asked for the watch or money. He was one of the aristocracy of the South. All good men dislike rascals, but they loathe and detest a *sneak* and *liar*.

At Gordonsville we were examined by the provost marshal, who deprived us of our shelter tents, blankets, valuables, and everything calculated to make a soldier, especially a prisoner, comfortable. All articles were taken from us that afterwards would have rendered our days of confinement, to an extent, supportable. We were taken by way of Gordonsville to prevent us from falling into the hands of our cavalry; a few days previous, they having rescued several hundred of our prisoners. At this place we were put in a dark, damp cellar,—all huddled together like swine,—some standing in pools of stagnant water, others sitting in filth. Frogs, lizards, toads, reptiles, rats, and huge spiders, were holding high carnival in this unhealthy, dreadful abode. Corn meal was issued to us, but no cooking utensils, (these useful articles had been taken from us,) nor had we wood to kindle a fire, if we had possessed a place to prepare the meal. Many ravenous men ate the meal raw, to sustain life. It was *rebel* conduct—systematic barbarity. From Gordonsville we were moved (had we not, all would have died from the effects of the poisoned atmosphere,) to Lynchburg, by way of Richmond.

> "What art thou, life, so dearly lov'd by all?
> What are thy charms that thus the great desire thee,
> And to retain thee part with pomp and titles?
> To buy thy presence, the gold-watching miser
> Will pour his mouldy bags of treasure out,
> And grow at once a prodigal. The wretch
> Clad with disease and poverty's thin coat,
> Yet holds thee fast, though painful company."

Libby Prison, Richmond, Va.

CHAPTER III.

Libby Prison—Vermin and "Skirmishing"—The Rebel Joke—Belle Isle—The Bloodhound—Rebels Wearing Uncle Sam's Clothing—Hostages—Foote—Castle Thunder—Colonel Streight and his Escape—Plot for the Capture of Richmond—Minstrels—Justice.

> "A prison! heaven's, I loathe the hated name,
> Famine's metropolis, the sink of shame,
> A nauseous sepulchre, whose craving womb
> Hourly inters poor mortals in its tomb;
> By ev'ry plague and ev'ry ill possess'd,
> Ev'n purgatory itself to thee's a jest;
> Emblem of hell! nursery of vice,
> Thou crawling university of lice."

I am going to tell you a few facts about the noted blackhole of the rebels, Libby Prison, Richmond. Though much has been related of the sufferings of our brave boys at this place, and on Belle Isle, half the dark, bloody, horrible scenes have not been made known, nor ever will; but the eye of the great God, who seeth all things, hath witnessed the fiendish atrocities perpetrated in the cimmerian dungeons of the Rebel Government's pet prison "Libby." It is a three story brick warehouse, low roof, divided into large rooms for the keeping of hundreds. The ceiling is not high. Warehouses in our cities are generally clean; not so with this one, which is extremely filthy, with no ventilation. The heart droops looking at the exterior, which is cheer-

C

less and funereal-like. The windows are very narrow, small and well guarded with bars. It looks more like a trap than a cage. It is surrounded by dilapidated shanties, and the canal runs behind it. The guards pace their beats around the building, anxious for a "shot" at some sickly hero who may stagger to the window for a breath of air. The office is on the first floor, and the damp cells under the building; the reeking sinks at the end of each room. The vermin sally forth from the cracks and give battle night and day. There were other prisons in Richmond, but Libby was the "darling" for officers.

When officers first enter prison they are inclined to be fastidious, and somewhat delicate about eating their peck of dirt, and "skirmishing" or hunting "grey-backs" in the presence of others. In a day or two, they no longer blush at their nudity, but pull the garment off, and enter into the spirit of murdering, without mercy, the disturbers of their peace and happiness. Once I noticed an officer who had entered prison very uneasy. I could not understand the cause of his restlessness, but attributed it to a nervous disposition. He sat or stood up all night. In the morning, by the first streak of light, the new-comer was the earliest bird to attack the enemy. I had the secret; he neglected to take a "skirmish," and so lost his rest. He was cured of his shame. Whatever scruples he had yesterday, about engaging in so *indelicate* an operation as "killing," were gone now.

To be able to live in any kind of peace, a close and constant examination of every part of the clothing was necessary. Every place was alive with "grey-backs." None of the officers possessed surplus clothing, so that the greatest economy had to be observed in washing, or it would wear out; and this was a dark feature in our prison life, with the prospect of a long imprisonment ahead. During the entire day, Generals, Colonels, and subalterns, were to be seen in earnest contest with the small but troublesome host.

A celebrated officer was one day sitting looking for the enemy, when a rebel officer entered, and attempted to get off a sarcastic joke. All present enjoyed a laugh at the expense of the Confederate.

Rebel—"Why, General, you are lousy?"

General—"No, I'm not; it's my shirt!"

He never tried to be smart again. Here is prison poetry:

> "Tell me not, in mournful number,
> Prison life is but a dream;
> 'Tis but little we can slumber,
> Swarms of lice in every seam."

The men were confined on Belle Isle, the civil and State offenders in Castle Thunder. These places were furnaces of affliction for the lovers of the Union who fell into the hands of the chivalry. In Castle Thunder hundreds were handcuffed, maimed, tortured, hung and shot, whipped until the weary soul winged its way to the Creator, glad of flight from earth. Noble martyrs! At the latter place there was a huge blood-hound called "Hero," that more than once had been turned into the cells of Union prisoners, and tore the life from sickly men who could not have survived the best of treatment.

For a long time during the winter of 1863, there was no general exchange, and our poor boys on Belle Isle experienced all the hardships nature can endure. To mitigate their sufferings, the kind-hearted people of the North, the Sanitary and Christian Commissions, and United States Government prepared large boxes of clothing, having made a mutual agreement with the Rebels to deliver the articles to the freezing heroes, and sent them to Richmond. One-eighth of the garments were never placed in the hands of our soldiers. The guards, and Rebels around Richmond, helped themselves. The officers commanding the prisons gloried in the robbery, and would strut in and out of jail with haughty and overbearing pride, dressed in suits of blue. One officer was placed in a dungeon for telling a rebel he was wearing Uncle Sam's uniform. Papers were appropriated and letters never delivered. Boxes of eatables, if given to the owner, were stale and mouldy. They had lain for months in the storehouse before delivery, the Rebel officers having stolen the delicate portions. The owner of a box would occasionally be sent for, and told to empty his goods into a blanket. Canned fruit, oysters, butter, etc., goods that required to be kept air-tight, were punched with the bayonet and promiscuously mixed—spoiled. Nothing was given to the owner fit for the stomach.

I became acquainted with several officers held as hostages, and who, for punishment in an attempt to escape, were confined for months in a subterranean cell under Libby. Their beards and hair were long and matted. One officer's beard had rotted from the effects of damp and mould. Another lost his eyesight on coming to the light of heaven, after the long confinement in midnight darkness. There was little flesh on their limbs or bodies. They were living skeletons. The twenty-four hour ration was greedily eaten at once. They had a celebration, in pic-nic style, when a rat was caught, which was eagerly devoured.

God only knows what these staunch hearts endured for the Union. They became acquainted with suffering's actual definition. If Jeff. Davis did not know of the inhuman treatment of Union soldiers only a few squares from his residence, he neglected his duty to the bogus concern he represented, which would make him, besides a traitor to his country, a renegade to the rebels. It has been demonstrated within the last few weeks that the Southern government endorsed a scheme to systematically starve our men. Major Turner, a notorious villian, who had charge of Libby, let no opportunity escape to withhold food, abuse, maim, and shoot prisoners in his charge. It has been proven against the rebels that rather than our men should rescue their starving companions from Libby Prison, they were to be blown up. Kegs of gunpowder were placed under the building, and the fiends were to send into eternity, without warning, the helpless captives whom they would not feed. No more consummate, blood-thirsty rascality has ever been exhibited by any people.

The Rebel senator Foote has contributed his testimony to the inhuman treatment our prisoners received. But the people of the North or the civilized globe required no proof of the hellish barbarities inflicted upon them. Nearly fifty thousand graves of Union soldiers around the hells and pens of the fiends in the South is sufficient evidence to condemn their damnable conduct. This is what the chivalric man of the South says:

"Touching the Congressional report referred to, I have this to say: A month or two anterior to the date of said report, I learned, from a Government officer of respectability, that the prisoners of war then confined in and about Richmond were suffering severely for want of provisions. He told me further, that it was manifest to him *that a systematic scheme was on foot for subjecting these unfortunate men to starvation; that the Commissary General, Mr. Northup (a most wicked and heartless wretch), had addressed a communication to Mr. Seddon, the Secretary of War, proposing to withhold meat altogether from military prisoners then in custody,* and to give them nothing but bread and vegetables, and that Mr. Sedden had *endorsed the document containing this recommendation affirmatively.*"

The South may rave and bluster, and attempt to refute the charge, but a good God overthrows their falsehoods and brings to light the actions of these followers of Satan.

There have been noble hearts in the South who have stood by the Union cause and have suffered martyrdom in devotion to their country. Men have been dragged from home and family to do service in an army they loathed, whose spirits and feelings still clung to the old flag, their fathers' emblem of happiness and prosperity. Castle Thunder was the receptacle, the living death-chamber of these bold, fearless men, who advocated their country's unity and welfare. All honor to their name. May the United States provide for those who have survived Southern ferocity.

"The terrible testimony of this Castle Thunder is an everlasting stigma upon the Southern cause. In the new commandant's room lay the record left behind by the Confederates. Its pages made one shudder.

These are two of its infamous entries:

"George Barton—giving food to Federal prisoner of war; forty lashes upon the bare back. Approved. Sentence carried into effect July 2."

"Peter B. Innis—passing forged Government notes; chain and ball for twelve months; forty lashes a day. Approved."

In an inner room are some fifty pairs of balls and chains with anklets and handcuffs. Within are two condemned cells, perfectly dark—a faded flap over the window peep-hole—the smell from which would knock a strong man down. In their centre lies the sink, ever open, and the floors are sappy with uncleanliness. To the right a door leads to a walled yard not forty feet long, nor fifteen wide, overlooked by the barred windows of the main prison, and by sentry boxes upon the wall top. Here the wretched were shot and hung in sight of their trembling comrades. The brick wall at the foot of the yard is scarred by balls and bullets which first passed through some human heart and wrote here their testimony. The gallows had been suspended from a wing in the ledge above. This little yard, bullet-marked, close, and shut off from all sympathy, is the ghastliest spot in the world. Up stairs, in Castle Thunder, there are two or three large rooms, barred and dimly lit, and two or three series of condemned cells, pent up and pitchy, where, by a refinement of cruelty, the ceiling has been built low so that no man can stand upright. Here fifteen or twenty were crowded together, and in the burning atmosphere they stripped themselves stark naked, so that when in the morning the cell-doors were opened they came forth as from the grave, begging for death. There are women's cells, too; for this great and valiant government recognized women as belligerents, and locked them up close to a sentry's cartridge, so that in the bitterness of solitude they were unsexed, and railed and blasphemed like wanton things. The pavements before the jail were trodden by remorseless guards, who shot at every rag fluttering from the cages, and all this little circle of death in life was enacted close to the light river and under the cover of that Capitol where criminal treason held the sinews of war to wring from a reluctant Union an arrogant independence."

Notwithstanding the strict guard kept by the commandant of Libby, Colonel Streight, a gallant and gentlemanly officer, with a large number of prisoners made their escape by tunneling from the basement, going down the chimney and working in the night. The Rebels hated Streight. He told them too many truths, which were not complimentary to their civilization. He was held as hostage and confined in a cell, where he was subjected to barbarity and outrage. The Richmond officials were greatly mortified and made every effort to recapture him. They said they would rather have lost half the prisoners around the city than the "hell-hound" Streight. But a kind Providence delivered him from the hands of his tormentors.

At one time there was a plot between the officers in Libby and men on Belle Isle to force the guard and capture Richmond, take Jeff. Davis prisoner and destroy the government property. By some means the rebels found it out. Some officers believed there was a spy among them; for the night the attempt was to be made, a brigade of infantry and a battery of artillery patroled the streets.

Performances were given at Libby that relieved many of the sad, weary prison hours. Some who had money bought themselves out of this den of filth and suffering. But I must go on to other prisons; the true story of Libby would fill volumes.

May God put it into the hearts of those who try such men as Jeff. Davis and Turner, to deal out justice to them. If not, every soldier will feel his cheeks crimson at the thought of his trials and the loss of his companions, when murder and treason go unpunished.

> "The land wants such
> As dare with vigor execute the laws.
> Her fester'd members must be lanc'd and tented:
> He's a bad surgeon that for pity spares
> The part corrupted till the gangrene spread,
> And all the body perish: he that's merciful
> Unto the bad, is cruel to the good."

CHAPTER IV.

Boy Heroes—Bravery—An Exhibition—Southern Ladies—"Down with the Traitor"—The Drunken Confederate Major—Pick pockets and Thieves—Cheerfulness Necessary to Health.

> "In death's kindly bosom our last hope remains—
> The dead fear no tyrants, the grave has no chains!
> On, on to the combat! the heroes that bleed
> For virtue, for mankind, are heroes, indeed.
> And, O! even if Freedom from this world be driven
> Despair not—at least we shall find her in heaven.
> On death's kindly bosom our last hope remains—
> The dead fear no tyrants, the grave has no chains."

I believe there has never been a war waged by any people in which there were so many youths engaged as in the late one. In some regiments there have been companies composed entirely of young persons—all in their teens. Mere children have battled with as noble spirit as the hardiest veterans of Napoleon's campaigns. They have stood up to the work of loading and firing with as determined a will as the tall Vermonter, muscular back-woodsman, enlightened Middlestatesman, or persevering and fearless Western man. Their tenacity, courage, and endurance on the high places of the field have become historic. At the battle of Gaines' Farm, on the Peninsula, there was a boy, fifteen years of age, in my company, who had received three wounds, but refused to leave the field until he fainted from the loss of blood, and was carried off.

A young man from Worcester, a private in the Fifty-seventh Massachusetts Regiment, in the battle of Cold Harbor, a year ago, was hit by a ball in the chin, which badly fractured the bone, and tore out several teeth. Another ball hit the right shoulder and fractured the shoulder-blade and remains undiscovered. The third ball passed through his abdomen, and brought him to the ground. His companions dragged him to a hole, where his body and head could not be seen by the enemy; but his legs being exposed, one ball passed through the calf of his leg, another cut a deep groove through his shin, another cut through the top of the instep, and another carried away the next to the great toe. He lay in the hole all day, and was then taken prisoner, and starved for several months, yet this young man is now in Worcester, erect and in good health, and not perceptibly lame. His name is E. P. Rockwood.

The claim of Missouri to have the youngest soldier is disputed by the Keystone State. Henry Weidensaul, a native of Morgantown, Berks Co., Pa., when fourteen years of age, entered the Forty-sixth Pennsylvania Infantry, and participated in the battles of Winchester, Cedar Mountain, Chancellorsville, Gettysburg, Resaca, Dallas, Kenesaw and Peach Tree Creek; was wounded for the first time in the last named fight, and re-enlisted last winter with the greater part of his regiment. He was seventeen years of age on the 1st of July last. Never was there a braver young man went forth to battle for our rights than the subject of this sketch. Leaving a comfortable home to brave the hardships of the battle-field, at the age of fourteen years, was enough to daunt more rugged, but not braver spirits. At the battle of Cedar Mountain he displayed such heroic courage and daring that he won the admiration of all the officers and men of his regiment. After being pierced by a ball through the hand, he could not be persuaded to go to the rear, but kept his place until the battle was over. The War Department could not do a nobler act than to commission this young hero, as he has fairly won promotion by his many deeds of valor.

In the same car with me, on the route to Lynchburg, was a boy seventeen years of age, wounded in the shoulder. It was his seventh wound. One ball had passed through his body. The rebel officer refused to allow him to procure water to wash his wound. His prayer was that he would soon be released, and live long enough to fire another shot at the scoundrels.

Here is another record of a gallant youth:

Stoel S. Putman, a youth fourteen years old, who was for some time employed in the editorial rooms of the *Herald* office, enlisted in New York, in the Brooklyn Fourteenth Regiment, in February, and was sent to Culpepper, Va. He was in all of General Grant's battles, from the Wilderness to Petersburg. At the battle of Spottsylvania he was taken prisoner; but, not admiring the companionship into which he had been forced, he jumped from the rebel rifle-pits and made his escape, amid a shower of bullets, rejoining his regiment, and using his musket until the close of the fight. While charging on the batteries at Petersburg he was shot in the body, the ball passing entirely through him, within an eighth of an inch of the heart. After the usual necessary delays, he was taken to the Lincoln General Hospital, in Washington, with nothing on him but his drawers, jacket and an old rebel gray cap. He recovered from his wounds, but he is now (having just turned his fifteenth year) lying at the government hospital at Newark, N. J., suffering from a severe pistol shot wound through the knee joint, which, however, was accidentally received. We think we hazard nothing in saying that he is at least the youngest man in the ranks from the State of New York.

The following touching ballad relates the story of a brave boy's heroism in the fearful fight before Vicksburg, on May 19th, 1863, and shows a devotion by a delicate boy to the cause as pure and noble as has ever been shown by the bravest hero of a hundred battles:

While Sherman stood beneath the hottest fire
   That from the lines of Vicksburg gleamed,
The bomb-shells tumbled in their smoky gyre,
   And grape-shot hissed, and case-shot screamed;
     Back from the front there came,
     Weeping and sorely lame,
   The merest child, the youngest face,
   Man ever saw in such a fearful place.

Stifling his tears, he limped his chief to meet;
   But when he paused, and tottering stood,
Around the circle of his little feet
   There spread a pool of bright, young blood.
     Shocked at his doleful case,
     Sherman cried, "Halt! front face!
   Who are you? Speak, my gallant boy!"
   "A drummer, Sir:—Fifty-Fifth Illinois."

"Are you not hit?" "That's nothing. Only send
   Some cartridges: our men are out;
And the foe press us." "But, my little friend"——
   "Don't mind me! Did you hear that shout?
     What if our men be driven?
     Oh, for the love of Heaven,
   Send to my Colonel, General dear!"
   "But you?" "Oh, I shall easily find the rear."

"I'll see to that," cried Sherman; and a drop
   Angels might envy dimmed his eye,
As the boy, toiling towards the hill's hard top,
   Turned round, and with his shrill child's cry
     Shouted, "Oh, don't forget!
     We'll win the battle yet!
   But let our soldiers have some more,
   More cartridges, Sir,—calibre fifty-four!"

At Lynchburg, a large town in Virginia, the militia took charge of us. They were men who had never seen service, and displayed their little authority with a zeal that brought smiles to the faces of old soldiers. These men had never been to the front, and were the most tyrannical tools who had charge of us while in Virginia. One of the citizens to whom I had given a cup to bring me some water, was arrested and placed in jail for aiding and sympathizing with Union soldiers. We were paraded through the streets of the town as if we were wild animals; all the people turned out to see the exhibition. The females smiled on the Home Guards and shook their closed hands at the captives; others contented themselves with dipping snuff and chewing tobacco. These are accomplishments of Southern ladies. The contrast between the rebels and prisoners, in manly bearing, on the display, was in favor of the latter, if they were hatless and shoeless and had their clothing stolen. They looked like men alongside of the scare-crows guarding them. One officer commenced to sing "Down with the Traitor;" others joined; in a few minutes all the prisoners were singing as loud as they could bawl; to us it was as good as a feast to see the angry Johnnies. A concourse of darkies followed us to the prison, who evidently pitied our condition, and knew we were the true friends of their race South. One of the colored men was knocked down for giving some tobacco to a prisoner.

A rebel major who had been imbibing the spirits of some of his Southern friends made his appearance, and in the language of Billingsgate poured out the vials of his wrath on our heads; he cursed us for Yankees, and said the Lord would destroy every mudsill, not only in the North, but in the universe. We had come down there to deprive them of their niggers, but in a few months we would all be keeping the Devil and old John Brown company in a warmer place than the South. Once he fell down, but jumping up and balancing himself, he shouted, foaming at the mouth like a dog possessed of the hydrophobia, "We'll burn New York and Philadelphia next week." The citizens of this inland town cheered the drunken orator, and cried "Good, good!" every time he hiccoughed and yelled his abuse on the heads of the unarmed, helpless and fatigued captives. He was one of the fire-eaters of the "sunny South." A gentleman who labored to prove the black man was an animal who had no rights, and for punishment should be put to death; one of those who spoke of the "last ditch," but run when danger threatened.

We were placed in the second story of a large building on the main street. That night we received no food, as we had been guilty of singing a Yankee hymn on the streets. O, Southern inhumanity! Our daily ration for the next week we remained here was a small piece of corn-bread, half-cooked, with a piece of pork you could scarcely see. I made two meals out of mine, but only lived. Here I saw a negro of my regiment, who had cooked for an officer; he had been outrageously abused. When he was captured they attempted to kill him. He was shot in the breast, and had a bayonet wound in the side. Poor fellow; he must have died. O, Southern chivalry! Up stairs were confined rebel deserters, thieves, pickpockets, and men for every species of crime and villainy. They made night hideous with noise. In the yard working was to be seen a slave as white as any of my readers; also a very black boy, with long, straight, *red* hair. About the time we were removed from here, the rations grew smaller, and had we remained at this place, many would have died of starvation. One at a time, under guard, was allowed to visit the yard. This was horrible cruelty to those who were sick with diarrhœa. We kept our spirits up by singing and speech-making, which somewhat relieved the monotony of our prison life. Those who allowed their hearts to sink never lived. The prisoner who took matters easy, possessed a lively imagination and a cheerful disposition, dragged through the weary time with less injury to the system. The cheerful smile and ready joke had a wonderful effect in sustaining the constitution.

> "A prison is a house of care,
> A place where none can thrive,
> A touchstone true to try a friend,
> A grave for one alive."

CHAPTER V.

Rebel Humanity—Death—Home—Mother—Three Officers Escape—The Fire eater—Danville—Jeff. Davis—Guards—Water—Food—Hope.

> "None to watch near him—none to slake
>   The fire that in his bosom lies,
> With ev'n a sprinkle from that lake,
>   Which shines so cool before his eyes.
> No voice well-known through many a day,
>   To speak the last, the parting word,
> Which, when all other sounds decay,
>   Is like a distant music heard.
> That tender farewell on the shore,
> Of this rude world, when all is o'er
> Which cheers the spirit, ere its bark
> Puts off into the unknown dark."

From Lynchburgh to Danville we were conveyed in box cars, as many as eighty or ninety being placed in a car. The prisoners were actually piled in on each other. These cars had been used in the transportation of animals; before our entrance into them they had not been cleaned or swept, and were in a repulsive state of filthiness. There were no windows, holes, or boards knocked off to admit air, As the weather was uncomfortably warm, these cars were almost as hot as bake-ovens. At times we were switched off on another track to allow the regular train to pass. We were in all respects treated like cattle; only worse, as we received neither food nor water. The successful farmer always looks to the wants of his stock. It took over twenty-four hours for a journey which should have been accomplished in three for the sake of humanity. In the car I was, two soldiers fainted. The want of a pure atmosphere sickened all of us. It was Southern mercy to place prisoners in this suffocating furnace. Guards were on the top of the car, but two of them filled up the only door which would have admitted some air. In one of the other cars a soldier died. He was from New Hampshire. Poor boy! The soul's flight must have been a relief; freed from torture, we sincerely hope to enjoy the company of the redeemed in paradise, where there are no rebels. Ah! it is heart-breaking to see one of your soldier companions die in the hands of a brutal foe; with no father present to give a parting word, or kind sister to cheer and soothe the escaping spirit, or loving mother to kiss the death-damp from the pallid brow.

Just before reaching Danville three officers made their escape by ripping off a loose board from the car, and jumping out whilst the train was in motion. It was night and the moon half full, but there were large clouds drifting to and fro, that every few minutes obscured her light, favoring the adventurers in their exit through the small opening. I was just about to take my departure and run the risk of reaching our lines, about one hundred miles away, when the moon emerged from beneath a cloud and cast her pale light on the scene, and at the same time the whistle signalled for Danville. In a a few seconds we were in the city. I felt very low in spirits. I was sick at heart. I had made up my mind to escape the first opportunity, as there was no exchange going on, and it was starvation and death by inches to remain in the hands of the rebels. I thought I had let pass the most fortunate opportunity that might ever take place. We were placed in line to be counted, after emerging from our loathsome dog-kennel. The rebel officer who had charge of us, jumped and floundered like a fish out of water. He counted us over at least a dozen times. He marched us a few paces and halted, then back and counted us again. He cursed and damned every Yankee living and dead. He told his men to shoot the first abolitionist that moved. We were all highly amused, and his great anger increased our mirth. One officer could not contain his feelings and laughed outright; the chivalric son of the South drew his sword and threatened us all with punishment, for our Northern conduct of laughing at his raging passion. Drawing himself up, and flourishing his blade, he said.

"Some of you 'uns run away; but they'll be caught, and made to suffer; if you laugh at me or my government, you'll have no food until you apologise. Move on!"

I thought of the lines:

> "O insupportable! O heavy hour!
> Methinks, it should be now a huge eclipse
> Of sun and moon, and that the affrighted globe
> Should yawn at alteration."

Danville is a small town, situated in Southern Virginia, on the northern bank of the river Dan, made notable as the place where Jeff. Davis issued his address of defiance and braggadocia against the North in his defeat, when he was a fugitive fleeing from justice, having neither a government, a capital, nor an army. But it was characteristic of this hoary-headed thief, traitor and murderer to still gull those who would listen to him. The great object of the arch-traitor was to secure a place of safety in a foreign land, and as self was his ruling passion, he continued to deceive until the object would be obtained. This town is the centre of the tobacco region, some fifteen millions of pounds of plug tobacco being annually manufactured here before the war. Its prosperity and glory have departed.

We were confined in a large warehouse near the river. The rooms were well ventilated, and had we been allowed the privileges of the yard, life would have been bearable as far as air and space were concerned. Our keepers were worse than those at Lynchburgh. They were ignorant and proud of the charge, and determined to make us suffer as much as lay in their power. I stepped to the window to take an observation of the surroundings of our prison, as also to inhale the pure air, when one of the rascals fired at me. He was not a good shot, or an ever-watchful Providence pointed the rifle, for the ball lodged in the wood work of the window two feet above my head. As *looking* was dangerous, few enjoyed the luxury of a peep. The water was unhealthy and bad and caused many to complain of cramps in the stomach. No soap was issued, nor were there facilities for washing clothes, so that "skirmishing" occupied a good part of our time. We remained at this place almost a week, being supplied with rations that almost ran. A small piece of corn-bread, a thin slice of pork, two inches square, made the twenty-four hour meal; or meals, if the temptation was resisted not to eat all at once. It was a severe struggle between the mind and stomach.

How many thousands would die in despair if no star of hope brightened their path through the labrynths of life's journey. It sustains the shipwrecked sailor and dying soldier, the Christian and suffering prisoner.

> "And faint not, heart of man! though years move slow!
> There have been those that from the deepest caves,
> And cells of night and fastnesses below
> The stormy dashing of the ocean waves,
> Down, farther down than gold lies hid, have nurs'd
> A quenchless hope, and watch'd their time and burst
> On the bright day, like wak'ners from the grave."

CHAPTER VI.

No Exchange—Rebel Honor—The Southern Paradise—Salisbury and its Horrors—Patriotic Family—Maj. Gee—Starvation—The Cat—Lieutenant Davis Murdered—Vengeance—Charlotte—Columbia—Augusta—Bradford the Black-Leg—Baltimore Thugs.

> "O, Liberty, thou goddess, heavenly bright;
> Profuse of bliss, and pregnant with delight!
> Eternal pleasures in thy presence reign,
> And smiling plenty leads thy wanton train;
> Eas'd of her load, subjection grows more bright,
> And poverty looks cheerful in thy sight;
> Thou mak'st the gloomy face of nature gay,
> Giv'st beauty to the sun, and pleasure to the day."

Orders were received to convey us into the State of Georgia. The rebels said there would be no exchange; that our government had abandoned us; that the Confederates had proposed to exchange man for man and officer for officer, but an answer had never been returned; that we were hired mercenaries, and the Yankees did not care if we all died. There was not one officer but knew the Federal Government ever watched with jealous care our treatment, whilst in their hands, and would make a general exchange as soon as it could be effected with honor and principle. All knew the rebels had repeatedly broken the *cartel*, or agreement entered into governing the exchange of prisoners of war. Rebels taken on the coast, in the South, and the many thousands captured at Vicksburg and *paroled* not to take up arms until regularly exchanged, were again in the field fighting against their magnanimous conquerors. As prisoners of war were accumulating in Virginia, and their own large armies had to be fed, the subsistence coming from Georgia, and Florida, and Alabama, we would be forwarded to the latter States to eat, drink and be merry; to bask under the live-oak trees of the modern Eden, Macon; to live in pleasure until the war would be over, at the Southern paradise, Andersonville! We were sent to this promised land, where our armies could never penetrate, nor our cavalry make raids and devastate the only land of delight and liberty in the Western Hemisphere!

> "Day hath no more glory,
> Though he soars so high;
> Thine is all man's story,
> Live, and love, and die!"

The same style of cattle cars were employed in transferring us to the South, as used in conveying us from Lynchburg to Danville. All suffered in body and mind, on the long, fatiguing, slow journey, pent up, with scarcely standing room, in the small box cars, having no water and little food. Several Union soldiers died on the route. What did the rebels care? Our pain gave them pleasure.

We passed the Salisbury Prison, North Carolina, one of the Southern hells in which thousands of our dear comrades died of starvation, and satanic cruelty. It was a common stockade, heavily guarded. Major Gee had charge of this pen. He was one of the most cowardly scoundrels and murderers a good God ever allowed to breathe his pure air. To keep green in the memory of the people a family who have done and lost so much in behalf of the Union cause, and display what a man will do when dying of hunger, to prolong life, I print the following true but horrible recital, taken from the Harrisburg *Telegraph;*

"We were this morning favored with a visit from a brave soldier named John Fon Rodd, of Company A, Thirteenth Pennsylvania Cavalry, who is here awaiting the arrival of his regiment, to be discharged. Mr. Fon Rodd is a German, and a son of William Henry Fon Rodd, Esq., of Butztown, Pa. The father is eighty-nine years of age, and has lost *nine sons* in the war for the Union. Eight of these were killed in battle, and the other died of starvation, in the rebel pen at Salisbury. While a prisoner, the son last referred to actually *ate his right hand*, so great was his hunger. John, from whom we have obtained our information, is the *tenth* and youngest of the brothers, and he bears the scars of *eight wounds* received in battle. He, too, was for a time a prisoner at Salisbury, and was only released at the close of the war. His recital of the treatment of the starving prisoners fully confirms all the accounts that have heretofore been published of the Southern barbarism under which our men suffered. Upon inquiry, we learn from other sources, that Henry William Fon Rodd, the father of the *ten heroes*, has for many years been one of the most highly respected citizens of Butztown. Is there another man in the world who has sacrificed more sons upon the altar of our country than this aged German?"

Gee and the officials at Salisbury attempted many times to seduce the poor, hungry, naked captives from their allegiance to the old flag. Plenty of food and clothing were offered if they would swear allegiance to the Southern cause. Brave hearts, and hungry, dying men were insulted with his propositions. For days no food would be issued; then bringing in slices of meat and bread, the tempting devil would put the question:

"Will you enlist in the Confederate Army, receive clothing, a supply of good wholesome food, and go out of prison?"

"No," said the starving heroes, looking at the inviting food, with watery eyes and bursting heart. One time there were a few, to save their lives, and go to their companions in arms the first opportunity offered, consented to the ruffian's base proposition. As chances occurred they fled to our troops. Their patriotism was the same to Uncle Sam. The rebels never did put arms in their hands. The fire of Gettysburg still burned in their bosoms abiding a time to consume their tormentors. Life is sweet! Were they to blame? The United States Government has never called them to an account for the course pursued.

One day a cat jumped across the *dead-line* into the stockade; a rush was made, and a tussle ensued for a sumptuous dinner. The cat was cooked and divided among a few: starving men stood by envying the repast. In Salisbury a cat was luscious fare.

Lieutenant Davis, of the one hundred and fifty-fifth New York Volunteers, was shot—*murdered* near the dead-line. He was a good soldier and a harmless man, and when killed was inside the bounds prescribed to prisoners. The sentinel received a furlough for his atrocious act. Others were shot as they sat or lay inside the pen.

The poor boys, goaded by insults and driven to despair, and believing death to be a relief, one day made a charge on the dead-line and guards. Some of the rebel fiends bit the dust. Alarm was given, and a regiment that was about to leave the depot hurried up and poured a volley into the prison-pen. Cannon, loaded with canister, were fired into the sickly, unarmed captives. Many were killed, and order restored. Noble fellows! Death freed them! Death loosed their bonds, and raised them to a happier, better world. Ah, Major Gee, you were not only a foe, but a devil. He was killed not long since by a *Southern* man.

> "Villain, thou knowest no law of God or man;
> No beast so fierce but knows some touch of pity."

The cars stopped for the night at Charlotte, North Carolina, and we were allowed to get out of the cars, surrounded by a strong guard. It was a great relief to be able to stretch our limbs after being cramped for so long a time. We were told we could lie down in the field all night. I saw several Union people here, but was not allowed to talk with them. Several poor women came to sell us pies and cakes, but the officer having charge of us cleared them away, saying, "You are not permitted to sell to Yankees." A man advanced in years beat a negro for bringing a canteen of water to an officer. About sun-down one of the chivalry came along, and in a raging passion ordered us off his farm, crying, "No d——d Yankee living will sleep on my farm." We had to go into the cars again, where we put in a miserable night.

Next evening we passed through Columbia, South Carolina, amidst sarcastic remarks of women and angry looks of men, who were administering to the wants of a train of wounded rebels, that had preceded us. To have so many maimed men among them from late battle-fields excited their ire against us; and in various ways they manifested it.

We stopped at Augusta, Georgia, one day, in a cotton store-house. Captain Bradford, the provost marshall, took charge of us Ex-Governor Bradford, of Maryland, a loyal man, is his father. The son is a vicious rebel, and one of the most contemptible scoundrels who had charge of us. Some stinking bacon, covered with filth and vermin, was brought to us. One officer remonstrated, Captain Brady, Second Regiment New Jersey Volunteers, and said it would sicken us to eat it. Bradford said:

"It's good enough for d——d Yankees; if I had

my way, I'd hang them all—every mudsill North."

The Government should get hold of him, and hang him as an example.

There were many Baltimore gamblers, blacklegs, thieves and thugs doing duty at Augusta. At all times they were unmerciful towards our men. They were cowards, holding positions at the rear to murder prisoners.

CHAPTER VII.

Escape from the Rebels—Freedom, but Dangers—In the Woods—Plans—Negroes—The Loyal, Christian Slave—Race for Liberty—No Food—Blood-hounds—Recapture—No Mercy—Jail—A Fight with Rats.

> "From life without freedom, say, who would not fly?
> For one day of freedom, O! who would not die?
> Hark! hark! 'tis the trumpet! the call of the brave,
> The death-song of tyrants, the dirge of the slave.
> Our country lies bleeding—O! fly to her aid;
> One arm that defends is worth hosts that invade.
> From life without freedom, O! who would not fly?
> For one day of freedom, O! who would not die?"

During the tedious ride South, as yet no seasonable opening was presented for escape. The most favorable chances occur in the transfer to a different prison. There are generally so many to watch, and the guards have to proceed with the prisoners, that occasionally they become careless, if not sleepy. Through the different States our escort was changed, and many of them were not acquainted with the fact that Yankees played tricks.

There was no exchange going on, nor likely to be, and to be incarcerated in a foul and loathsome pen, to die of abuse and starvation by a process of refined cruelty made me sick at heart, and willing to engage in any desperate enterprise, having for its object escape and liberty. I had served three years, and at the time of my capture the regiment to which I belonged was going home. This fact, with reflections of the dear ones in the far-off North who awaited my coming, quickened my feelings of duty to country and relatives, to make a bold push for freedom. After leaving Augusta, and as day was drawing to a close, and when we thought all hope was gone, as we drew near the end of our journey, the desired opportunity took place.

About sun-down, the guards at the door of the box-car were relieved. The two substitued were as sleepy and ignorant looking beings as ever served a bad cause. They seemed as if they did not care whether the Confederacy lived or died, providing they had plenty to eat and drink. Colonel Higginbotham, the officer mentioned in the first chapter as rendering service at the battle of the Wilderness, Colonel Swift, Captains Brady, Logan, Telford and myself, matured a plan to get out of the clutches of the rebels.. A great many proposals were suggested. In the hurried whispers all were of one opinion that *force* must not be employed. The Southern heart, we knew, would show no mercy if we were caught, after using physical force in our escape. As soon as quite dark, Colonel Higginbotham and myself were to enter into a conversation with the guards, and take the caps off their rifles, whilst the others, with a pocket-knife, taking turns, were to cut a hole large enough for the exit of the body. For a long time we could not engage the attention of the guards; they were sullen and morose, and suspicious that all was not right. The Colonel being a judge of human nature, and possessing a large amount of wit, and the power of fascinating with a smooth, quick tongue, at length seduced the guards to become interested in his humor. Cutting the heavy boards of the car with a pocket-knife was very slow work, but the prospect of liberty stimulated the workers, and by midnight an aperture large enough for a man to squeeze through was made. I deprived one of the muskets of its cap, and the Colonel the other, whilst singing a comic song, so that they were unfit for immediate use. Although the train was travelling at the rate of twenty miles an hour, one after the other jumped into the unknown darkness, after hanging on the outside of the car a few seconds. Colonel Higginbotham who was a very stout man, large and muscular, with difficulty pressed his way through the hole. He received some injury in his fall. Colonel Swift leaped off where there was a high embankment. He fared the worst, receiving bad bruises in the shoulders and body in rolling over the rugged and uneven earth. One shot was fired by a guard on another car, but did no harm. To an extent we were now free. There were no miscreants close by us, always pointing a loaded gun at our bodies. O the rapture of our hearts to be once more free! Surrounded by dangers, but breathing God's pure, free air! Our joyous bosoms swelled with ecstacy, and we gave vent to our feelings in shaking hands, crying and laughing. From every lip went up to heaven a heart-felt "thank God."

We struck out into the woods to get away from the rail-road as far as possible before daylight, as tomorrow we would be pursued. An account of subsistence was taken, and it was found there was sufficient for twenty-four hours. There were eight in the party. To be able to get together, we arranged matters so as to assemble on the first man who leaped from the car; so far all worked well.

We travelled during the whole night. As the first streaks of day appeared in the east, a halt was made. A place was selected away from roads, convenient to water, and in the heart of a thick woods, among long grass and young trees. Our great fear was in meeting a white man. It was known to us the negro would prove true, and help us; but we had a repugnance for meeting even him, and would only seek his aid when necessity compelled. During the day we heard the sharp crack of a rifle, and every heart beat rapidly, whilst the earth was hugged as close as if we expected it to open and conceal us. Peering through the heavy foliage we discovered it to be a planter hunting. Once he came close by us, and our hearts could be heard beating. O the suspense, the agony of spirit during the time!

The fear and uncertainty of discovery! He passed on, then came relief; we breathed again. Each provided himself with a good stick. A leader was appointed and a system entered into to govern us until we should reach our lines. To avoid all dangerous places, picket posts, and situations where there would likely be a large number of guards, we would have to travel some two hundred miles. We should go around the right flank of the rebel army, and cross the Blue Ridge, and make for our western army; to travel in Indian file, in each other's tracks, and only at night, so as not to risk our liberty. Every care was to be observed in the minutest details. The woods and swamps were to be our hiding places, and no roads to be travelled if possible. We had no maps, but Colonel Higginbotham who had been a short time at Atlanta, before the war, possessed some knowledge of the country; although the North Star, in clear nights, was always our guide.

On the evening of the second day we had no food. It was too early in the season for potatoes or corn. It was found impossible to approach a planter's house during the night, on account of the many dogs. Accidently we passed by houses, and such yelping and barking of hounds and terriers was never heard North. Two went on an expedition for food, and providentially obtained some cornmeal and information. They approached a field cautiously, where there was a colored man working, and beckoned to him. He came and said:

"Lar's a heaven's; yees Yankees; glory to God; go off massas; if dey catch yees here, they kill yous!"

After dark the poor negro slave, stealing cautiously through by-paths, brought us provisions. For days these warm-hearted, generous, down-trodden people supplied our wants. Expeditions were always made to the colored people at nightfall, so that if an alarm was created, twenty miles could be gained and a hiding place selected by daylight. One evening it was arranged with an old slave man to bring us a bag of meal and a shote. We were resting quietly, and anxiously awaiting his coming, when two or three jumped to their feet and said, "We are discovered; here is a man on horseback." The alarm was momentary; it was the negro, but he brought bad news! His master had sent from Sparta, a town in Georgia, for his horse; the whole county was up in arms and a state of excitement, on account of a company of escaped and desperate Yankees prowling through the country. Stopping in his story he cried:

"Der dey cum; dey habe de hounds wid 'em! Be off! Be away!"

At the same moment, shouting men and yelping dogs could be heard some distance off. It was too true; the Southern miscreants had put the bloodhounds on our track. We doubt if savages ever did such a cruel wrong in all their vengeful hours? But this was the refinement of the South, the boasted enlightenment of the aristocracy, the chaste civilization of the chivalry, the Christianity of the slave-dealers! It was part of their religion to keep a good stock of blood-hounds, to track a negro and tear his life from him with the teeth of fierce dogs for running from the lash! The faithful, loyal slave, took us through swamps, across streams, along by-paths, guided us through woods for six miles. Before parting he asked us to step into a graveyard close by. He had risked his life for us, and why should we not comply with the request? Here this poor, unlearned slave, amidst tomb-stones, and graves, in the silence of night and in the "city of the dead," offered a prayer to the true God, for our deliverance from the hands of our foes, and our safe return to friends. It was a solemn and impressive scene, one long to be remembered—the slave's petition in the Georgia cemetery.

The race for liberty now began. All were weak for want of food. The prospect of freedom nerved every heart, and strengthened every limb. On, on we walked and ran, over rivers, and wading in swamps, resting for a moment, exhausted, then on again. At times the dogs could be heard yelping, then the pace was quickened. For hundreds of yards streams were waded to throw the dogs off the scent. Our pursuers were mounted. Two more nights, if Providence favored us, and we would be with our friends. For forty-eight hours we had not tasted food. Coming to a mulberry tree, two of the strongest climbed it and shook the luscious food to the earth. They were not eaten but devoured; strength returned, and freedom said, *On, on!*

> "*I do not starve*, not yet, not yet:
> But wait to-morrow! Famine will be here.
> In the meantime, we have still grim care,—(whose tooth
> Is like the tiger's—sharp)—lest dreams should fall,
> And shadow us with sweet forgetfulness."

Every man and boy, also some women, in three counties joined in the pursuit of the Yankees; messages were sent fifty miles ahead, in the direction we would be likely to take. Nearer and closer came the yelping hounds. On we struggled,—but the dogs were on the right track and the pursuers gained. Thus it was half the night. We were crossing a road about two o'clock in the morning, when several voices cried, "Halt! Surrender, you d——d Yankees or you are dead men." All was lost. There was a company of them armed, and it would be madness for a few unarmed men to resist. The dogs now came up, and would have torn us had not some of the more tender-hearted rebels interfered. Some of them said the dogs should bite us; we deserved killing anyhow. I made my retreat up a tree where the dogs could not follow me. Lieutenant Sutler got on a high rock just in time, minus some clothing, and the marks of a hound's teeth. Again prisoners; once more among cut-throats! Some of us were threatened with death, tied and sent to jail. I was confined

Re-captured.

in a filthy cell, the noxious vapors of which would have been the cause of my death in one week if I had not been removed. Although very sleepy from the fatigues undergone, I had to keep walking or making noise all night to prevent rats from attacking my person. Once I had a running fight, and came off victorious. A kind God brought me out of this terrible place alive; glory be to His name.

Though completely worn out, prostrated and sick in spirit, I received new strength as I feebly recited the beautiful lines:

> "The proudest motto for the young!
>   Write it in lines of gold
> Upon thy heart, and in thy mind
>   The stirring words enfold;
> And in misfortune's dreary hour,
>   Or fortune's prosperous gale,
> 'T will have a holy, cheering power—
>   'There's no such word as *fail*.'"

CHAPTER VIII.

Andersonville and its Butchers—Punishment for its Villainous Keepers—Justice—No Quarters—Food—Wood and Water—The Fiends, Winder and Wirz—The Hounds—Death and Suffering—The Hospital—Testimony—Brutality—No Mercy—God will Punish the Guilty.

> "The bugle's wild and warlike blast
> Shall muster them no more;
> An army now might thunder past,
> And they heed not its roar.
> The starry flag 'neath which they fought,
> In many a bloody day,
> From their old graves shall raise them not,
> For they have passed away."

I now come to the chapter of a prison, at which to relate its horrors the heart shrinks from the task, and the hand becomes palsied. The "Andersonville Pen" are words as familiar to every man, woman and child in the land as father and mother. There are none in the country, not even in the South, who will dispute the fact that the soldiers of the Union were starved by the thousands and murdered by the hundreds by relentless, unmerciful demons in the shape of men, at this slaughter-house in the South. It is past question that the Confederate authorities did deliberately, and with thoughts of murder in their hearts, perpetrate the awful enormity of torturing to death sixty or seventy thousand helpless but brave men; slain by a refined process of cruelty to which the savage and revolting atrocities committed during the Sepoy rebellion were merciful, and on their souls must rest the blood of this great multitude.

If the cruel Thugs of India, and the savage and relentless red men of the forest, could have witnessed the procession of emaciated forms, fleshless and walking skeletons, after release from the hands of their Southern keepers, their unfeeling natures would have been awakened with amazement, sympathy and pity for the victims sacrificed by a species of barbarity more refined and prolonged than they had ever committed, and more devilish than their bloody, dark and villainous hearts had ever thought of. At most, a few days' amusement and torture sufficed to appease their hardened bosoms against captives, and the knife or bullet put an end to their agony. Their benighted souls had never conceived the horrible idea of retaining them for years and starving them by inches, nor allowing soap or water to keep clean, so that vermin increased so fast that they eat the flesh off the ribs and bones of the unfortunate men. Their heathen hearts possessed this trait, if it can be called such, when compared to the fiendish jailors of Southern prisons: they never witheld food, or protracted for weeks and months the sufferings of their victims. But the enormous crime of maltreating, abusing, and starving United States soldiers, was committed by men who boasted of a superior civilization; who prided themselves on their gentlemanly qualities and elegant manners; who exulted in their refined feelings and polished education. The authorities have been active in starting the machinery of government in the Southern States, and pardoning the men who gave their wealth and influence, and raised their arms to destroy the best form of government the Lord had ever bestowed upon any people; and now the loyal men of the land, the million of scarred, weather-beaten and bronzed veterans who redeemed Columbia and saved the Republic, only ask for the same zeal and spirit to be employed in ferreting out and bringing to punishment the fiends who murdered their gallant fellow-citizens and soldiers at the prison-pens in the South. We profess to be a Christian nation. We live in a land of civilization, light, liberty and religion. Steamboats, railroads, telegraphs, churches, schools, colleges and printing presses, are to be found in every State, East and West, North and South, so that "he that runs may read." The eyes of the world have gazed with admiration on us for our great industry and progress, and our rapid advancement in knowledge and the arts and sciences. But ah! with all our education and light, in a portion of the land, throughout the Southern States, from seventy to eighty thousand helpless captives were actually starved to death. Starved to death—murdered by inches by men who were educated, and gloried in their graces and accomplishments. For such unparalleled crime against helpless men, every sentiment of respect and justice, every moral principle of our natures, cry out for swift and sure punishment, the most prompt and severe the law of the land affords. "An eye for an eye, and a tooth for a tooth." Could the scoundrels who perpetrated these dark acts be only made to suffer part of the terrible punishment inflicted on their victims, millions of honest hearts would say it was a righteous judgment. The blood of the martyred myriads calls for penal retribution against their unmerciful jailors. The people desire to see justice administered, nor will they rest satisfied until condign punishment is inflicted on the heads of villainous jailors, who murdered our poor, brave boys in Southern pens, stockades and slaughter-houses. "Thy mercy, O Lord, is in the heavens; and thy faithfulness reacheth unto the clouds." "Vengeance is mine, saith the Lord, and I will repay it."

The Andersonville prison was erected for enlisted men, and only a few officers were taken to this pen, who were recaptured after escape, or who desired to pass for privates, believing they would have a better opportunity among so many to get away from the rebels. The pen was about two hundred yards long, and one hundred wide. Some thirty-five thousand human beings were huddled together in this small space. It was a mean-looking stockade, about seventeen feet high, the posts being sunk in the ground some four or five feet. The ground selected was on the side of a hill, part of it being in a marsh. At the foot of the slope ran a small brook, not five feet wide nor half a foot deep. The position selected was such an one as fiends would pick out to accomplish the dark crime of which the cruel keeper of Andersonville stands charged. In the enclosure there were no tents, huts, barracks or houses, to protect the inmates from the scorching rays of a tropic sun of a Southern summer, or the cold and biting frost of a dreary winter. As prisoners came to the pen they were robbed of their clothing, blankets, shelter-tents, shoes, and even shirts. They were deprived of everything worth keeping that had previously escaped the eyes of those who had charge of them, and then put into the slaughter-house to run around like lost sheep. General Winder (the demon is dead) said: "I am going to establish a 'killing' depot; there will be more Yankees die this summer than have been shot by our soldiers since the battle of Bull Run!" Whilst living the rascal fulfilled his diabolical mission. Winder had charge of all the prisons east of the Mississippi. A Captain Henry Wirz had immediate command of the internal arrangements of the prison pen at Andersonville. This man was one of the most bloodthirsty brutes a wise Providence ever permitted to pollute his foot-stool. He was in his proper element when abusing, torturing and murdering the prisoners of whom he had charge. *By his orders hundreds were shot and thousands starved!* Poor creatures, who could scarcely walk, were put in the chain-gang, and fastened in the stocks, and kept there until their Creator released them from excruciating agony and awful suffering. Dying men were shot, whipped and scourged; taunted by their inhuman, relentless jailors until they fainted, and He who made them had compassion and called their souls from the hands of the barbarians. The truthful record of torture and inhumanity displayed by Pagan nations in all ages, from the murder of Abel to that of President Lincoln, shows some spirit of kindness when compared to the atrocities inflicted on unarmed captives at Andersonville. Blood-hounds were not only kept at the prison to track escaped prisoners, but they were hissed on and encouraged to bite, tear and devour the recaptured soldiers of the United States. Men have been shot in trees by the chivalry for spite, because their dogs could not reach the fugitives. This was the superior civilization of the South! Besides six regiments of infantry doing duty at this prison, there were some fifteen pieces of artillery always ready to open on the prisoners in case of an outbreak. About one-half of the camp drew raw rations, and did their own cooking, but were allowed little or no wood to cook them. Men were to be seen digging three or four feet down in the ground, with their hands, to procure a piece of the green root of a tree to make a fire to cook their meal and keep from starving. Many of the poor fellows were as black as negroes from the effects of the dirty pine smoke; water will not cleanse it from the skin, and not having soap, the dirt was completely ground into the flesh. Dirty, emaciated and almost naked, the poor men were a pitiful sight. Those who became too sick to hunt vermin died in a few days, actually *eaten up by lice!* The remainder of the prisoners received half-cooked rations, and fared the worst, as it was unfit to eat, and the twenty-four hour ration could be put away in the stomach in three or four mouthfulls. Stinking pork was issued, so full of maggots that it would walk. The daily ration was: half a pint of corn-meal, cob and all ground together; a quarter of a pint of some dirty kind of sorghum, (sickening stuff;) a piece of bacon you could only see from its moving with the aid of vermin; a quarter of a tea-spoonful of salt, and many days not any; some unclean peas, or hog beans were occasionally issued. The water used in washing, cooking and drinking was procured at the small run which passed through the stockade, and was so unclean as to be unfit for man or beast. There were no sanitary or police regulations established; no discipline among the thirty-five thousand; no system to drain the camp of its slop and filthy water; the garbage, offal, refuse and dirt of the whole prison passed into the stream that supplied all with water. The water at no time was suitable for cooking or drinking, and surely it was a running stream of disease, poison and death, when the foul matter of so many unfortunate beings floated into it. When it rained the inside of the pen presented the appearance of a clay road passed over by an army in wet weather; a sheet of soft mud, three, four and six inches deep through which the brave men of the Republic crept, reeled, staggered, fell and died.

The rebels made a pretence of keeping hospitals connected with the pen; but they were only pest-houses of corruption and death. They would not give to patients the medicine they possessed. The starved, naked and diseased prisoners lay in their filth and dirt on the hard ground, in sight of tons of hay and straw. The unmerciful brute, Wirz, said: "I am of more use to the Confederate Government than General Lee and his army, for I kill more d——d Yankees." The many thousands who died at Andersonville through want, neglect and disease maintained the principles of the government for which they went forth to battle. The bloody-minded Wirz and his associates could torture and kill with chain-gangs and stocks, but could not wring from Northern hearts their patriotism. Believing in the justness of their cause and a wise Providence, these poor prisoners could say:

> "Nail up my head on yonder tower,
>   Give every town a limb,
> And God who made shall gather them:
>   I go from you to him."

The effects of the inhuman treatment was visible in the faces and manners of hundreds of the captives: they wandered about the enclosure with haggard, down-cast looks, and glassy eyes; their mental faculties were gone; they had no reason; they crept, walked or staggered to the dead line, and were shot. *Eighteen* were shot in one day. God called out of their bonds and sufferings and the power of their vicious jailors eighteen souls in one day who were shot! As many as two hundred and ten died in one day. Dozens of the poor fellows were hung, the rebels said, for violating their parole, when their fingers had never touched pen or paper. A crowd of starved and naked men could be seen, in different parts of the prison, standing around the body of some brave man, waiting for the soul's flight, to carry it out of the prison, so that they might be able to gather the refuse and rotten wood lying around the outside of the stockade, to cook their scanty ration of dirty corn-meal and prolong burdensome lives.

There were desperate characters in the prison, who committed acts of violence, outrage and murder. Men, who never were honest or good in their manhood, became devils in this pandemonium. Surrounded by no moral or restraining influences, their natures became hardened to vice and crime.

For protection, the prisoners organized a police force, who caught six of the most desperate characters. They were tried by court-martial and hung.

The prayer-meetings and religious gatherings make *one* bright spot in the memory of every Christian who spent any time at the Andersonville Golgotha! Sergeant Benjamin N. Waddle, of Ohio, an old college friend, must receive the honor of being the first man to gather his dying comrades together to seek consolation at the throne of grace in worship and prayer. This noble and pure-minded man died at Annapolis on his way home.

> "They do not fail who fall
> In a great cause; the block may soak their gore,
> Their heads may sodden in the sun, their limbs
> Be strung to the city gates and castle walls;
> But their spirits walk abroad."

Prayer, singing and preaching was held two or three evenings in the week. Among those who stood up for Jesus were N. S. Cord, Sixteenth United States, Frank W. Smith, of Ohio, James C. Turner, of Pennsylvania, George Hovey, of Iowa, and Thomas Bourne, of Massachusetts, a Mr. Miller, of the Ninetieth Ohio Volunteers, and many others.

It is said by those who are entitled to respect for truthfulness that the bodies of twenty-three thousand Union soldiers are lying around the prison pen at Andersonville! The record of this slaughter-house would be incomplete if I were not to give to my readers the testimony of a few of the witnesses given in evidence at the trial of the murderer, Wirz, at Washington. From a sincere regard for the delicate and Christian feelings of those who will read this book, I will not pollute its pages with a description of the awful scenes that took place in this Southern Hades.

J. Nelson Clarke testified that he was taken as prisoner to Andersonville about the 28th of May, 1864, and confirmed the previous evidence as to the crowded and filthy condition of the stockade, the sufferings of the prisoners, the coarse, dirty and insufficient amount of rations, &c. In August of last year he counted one hundred and eighty-four dead men in the stockade. The witness mentioned the case of an insane soldier who wandered up and down by the stream, refusing to wear clothes, and who had not sense enough to know that he must cook his rations, and who ended his life by suicide. Another prisoner destroyed himself by hanging, having previously declared that he would rather die than remain in this stockade. Forty-one men in witness' company when captured were taken to Andersonville; twenty-two of them died, principally at that prison; he saw six men shot at different times; two of them he knew died; one of them extended his arm too far out over the dead line while dipping water out of the stream, when the sentinel fired; another of the prisoners happened to get slightly beyond the dead line, the sentinel fired, but instead of hitting him struck a man who was lying in a tent.

Martin E. Hogan testified as to his having been a

prisoner at Andersonville: the men were in a miserable condition, as bad as possibly could be: the men were so thick they could scarcely elbow their way; some lay in their own filth calling for water and crying for food, but no attention was paid to them; he also testified to other circumstances attending the prison, showing the miserable quality of the food and its injurious effects—such as half-baked corn bread, which was sour; the beef when it was furnished being of an inferior quality; men afflicted with scurvy would crawl upon the ground; the sight was horrible; very many were insufficiently clad, and, having no shelter, burrowed in the ground; as to hounds, he was brought back to prison through their agency; he had seen Captain Wirz with hounds trying to strike the trail of an escaped prisoner; for attempting to escape from prison about the 8th of October, 1864, after the most obscene abuse from Captain Wirz, he was fastened by the neck and feet, and remained there sixty-eight hours; he heard Captain Wirz give orders that he should not have food, but he did obtain food from paroled comrades who stole it for him; he had seen three comrades put in the stocks at the same time; one man was put in the stocks because he asserted his manhood by resenting the abuse of a Confederate soldier; when the prisoners were being removed from Andersonville to Millen, the witness saw Captain Wirz take a man by the collar because he could not walk faster; the man was so worn by disease that he could not; throwing the man on his back he stamped upon him with his feet; he saw the man bleeding, and he died a short time afterwards.

Here is the testimony of a Rebel surgeon, Dr. J G. Roy:

The men presented the most horrible specimens of humanity he ever saw; a large number of them were affected with the worst form of scurvy; he attributed the sickness to long confinement, exposure, and the absence of the comforts of life; there were maggots in the swamp near the hospital, the malaria from which had a most fatal effect upon the patients; the insects, or white ants with wings, were such as result from decayed animal and vegetable matter; they were so numerous that it was dangerous for a man to open his mouth at sundown. The witness had heard there was a deadline, and one of his patients had been killed.

Oliver B. Fairbanks, of the 9th New York Cavalry, testified that he was a prisoner at Libby, and afterwards taken to Andersonville; the father of the witness died in prison, and made a statement to him about ten minutes before he died; the witness placed his hand on the paper and wrote what was now presented to the Court, as follows:

"Camp Sumpter, Andersonville, Ga., August 27th, 1864.—Oliver—I die from sheer starvation, and don't for the world tell your mother of the awful condition which I am compelled to die in." Signed Richard Fairbanks.

Thornton B. Turrell, 72d Ohio regiment, testified that he was taken to Andersonville on the 19th of June; Wirz threatened the men, using vile language; a man who showed Capt. Wirz his ration of corn bread, and asked whether better could not be furnished, was met with the response, "d—— you, I'll give you bullets for bread;" there was not sufficient accommodation for one-twentieth part of the prisoners; the swamp was more than a foot deep with human excrement, and this spoiled the water in the wells; on one occasion he saw forty-five corpses in the dead house, on another, seventy-five or a hundred; the bodies were thrown into the creek like dead hogs, fifteen or twenty being a load.

William Willis Scott testified to the cruelty of Captain Wirz. In the latter part of August, a sick man sitting on a bank, asked Captain Wirz to be be sent to the hospital, when the latter cursed the invalid and struck him a violent blow over the head. The man went into his tent and died a day or two after. The witness mentioned another case, where one of the guard threw a brickbat and struck Wirz on the shoulder. Wirz, without stopping to make inquiry, drew his revolver and shot a Union man.

Dr. Burrows certified that at Andersonville prisoners were arrested for buying green corn, which the guard took away from them. Corn is an anti-scorbutic in cases of scurvy, and is a useful diet. The slops from the cook houses were thrown into the stream which ran through the prison, the exhalations from which were horrible and very unhealthy. Besides, the sinks overflowed, owing to the rains, rendering the premises still more intolerable. Human bodies sometimes lay unburied for three days. The stench was terrible, sensibly affecting the atmosphere, and was worse than any dissecting room. Complaints of these things were frequently made to headquarters; dead men were in the morning frequently found among the living. The largest number of deaths in the stockade for one day, in August, 1864, was two hundred and seven. The witness found Captain Wirz in charge of the prison when he went there, and left him there at the time he made his escape. Rations were cut off from the entire number of thirty thousand prisoners for an entire day, owing to alleged offences of a few others; the witness remembered that Wirz said to him he (Wirz) was of more service to the Confederate Government than any poor rebels in front.

The rebel Inspector of Prisons, D. L. Chandler, says of the scoundrel Winder.

My duty requires me respectfully to recommend a change in the officer in command of the post, Brigadier General J. H. Winder, and the substitution in his place of some one who at least will not advocate deliberately, and in cold blood, the propriety of leaving them in their present condition until their number has been sufficiently reduced by death to make the present arrangements suffice for their accommodation; who will not consider it a matter of self-laudation, boasting that he has never been inside the stockade—a place, the horrors of which it is difficult to describe, and which is a disgrace to civilization.

The dark crime of starving helpless men will cling to the Southern name and go down to posterity as the most atrocious act perpetrated in ancient or modern times.

There was one thought that cheered the prisoners in their misery and woe, it was that their comrades would release them. When Atlanta was taken and Sherman's victorious columns were pushing on, *hope* brightened every eye, and gladdened every heart. Though they did not sing the words, the sentiment of the beautiful song entitled "The Prisoner's Hope" gave momentary joy and happiness:

In the prison cell I sit,
  Thinking, mother dear, of you,
And our bright and happy home, so far away;
  And the tears, they fill my eyes,
Spite of all that I can do,
  Tho' I try to cheer my comrades and be gay.

CHORUS.

Tramp! tramp! tramp! the boys are marching,
  Cheer up comrades they will come;
And beneath the starry flag
  We shall breathe the air again,
Of the free land, in our own beloved home.

In the battle front we stood,
  When their fiercest charge they made,
And they swept us off a hundred men or more;
  But before we reach'd their lines,
They were beaten back dismayed,
  And we heard the cry of vict'ry o'er and o'er.

CHORUS—Tramp! &c.

So within the prison cell,
  We are waiting for the day
That shall come to open wide the iron door;
  And the hollow eye grows bright,
And the poor heart almost gay,
  As we think of seeing home and friends once more,

CHORUS.—Tramp! &c.

CHAPTER IX.

Macon Military Prison—Stockade—Guards—"Look Out for the Dead Line!"—Quarters—Washing—Food—Wood-Water—Rations and Cooking Utensils—Yankee Ingenuity—Sutlering—Insults—The Boys are Coming!

> "Father, look up and see that flag,
> How gracefully it flies;
> Those pretty stripes,—they seem to be
> A rainbow in the skies."
>
> "It is your country's flag, my son,
> And proudly drinks the light;
> O'er ocean's waves, in foreign climes,
> A symbol of our might."

My next entry into a rebel prison was at Macon, a large town about the centre of Georgia. After undergoing a thorough search, and receiving some abuse for giving the Confederate Government so much trouble, I was ushered into the presence of fourteen hundred Federal officers, of all ranks, from Lieutenant to General. From the experience I had gained while in the Confederacy, I managed to secrete my notes, or diary, and a sister's Testament. All were huddled together like brutes, without method or system, in a small space of ground, not three acres inside of the "dead line." From this enclosure nothing could be seen outside. The prison was a stockade, composed of heavy pine boards, twelve or fourteen feet high. On the outside a suitable platform was erected, on which the sentinels walked, and, at a glance, could see anything taking place inside of the inclosure. On the north side, close by the gate, and on the east side two twelve-pound brass cannon held a conspicuous place, to mow down the captives in case of an outbreak. In the latter part of June, fearing the vengeance of the suffering captives, three others were posted in the woods, in the rear of the camp, as supports.

Inside, twenty feet from the stockade, was the "dead line." True to its character, as its name signifies, death was the portion of any unfortunate who might fall against or touch it by accident. When any prisoner came too near the dead line, his companions would cry, "*Look out for the dead-line!*" He would jump as if bitten by a snake. The captive would unflinchingly face the belching cannon, but recoiled at the thought of being murdered by a vigilant, unmerciful foe. It was a common picket fence. It always marked the bounds of our prison. Between the stockade and "line" fires were lit at night, to enable the guards to see all that might take place, and inflict the death-penalty on any one who might come too near.

Near the centre of the enclosure there was a large dilapidated building, occupied principally by general and field officers for quarters. It was one of the filthiest places in the pen. All the sick crowded into it in the wet weather. Efforts were made to keep it clear of vermin and its sanitary condition respectable, but without success. From the steps of this building the mail was distributed, *when it came*, as also were religious services held. The rebels pretended to furnish lumber to build quarters, the prisoners erecting them; but, during the time I was here, there were hundreds who never had the least shelter from the weather; they lay out in the drizzling rain, and suffered from the burning heat of a Southern sun. The buildings, or sheds, put up held from seventy-five to one hundred. These sheds, or roofs, only answered the purpose of a shelter from the sun and rain. No lumber was furnished for bunks, and officers who had them obtained, or purloined, the material without consent. During my first month's stay in this prison, the ground was my bed, and the sky my only roof, in all kinds of weather. I had become inured to all kinds of hardships in my three years of soldiering, or this terrible exposure would have been the cause of my death. I did not have a blanket, but, fortunately, it was summer time, and I did not require much clothing. I had travelled so much, when I tried to escape, that my shoes were nearly worn out. For about eight weeks I did not have a shoe on my foot. At first my feet swelled, but gradually I became accustomed to go "barefooted."

A spring on the south side of the prison fur-

Wash-Day.

nished us with water, in the month of June; the water was good, but scarce. Three wells were then dug and wooden pumps put in. Wood was issued daily; one officer for ten men was allowed to go out under guard and bring in all he could, which must suffice until the next issue. There were days on which we could not cook for lack of wood. To keep clothes clean they should be scalded in the wash; but this we could not do, having scarcely enough wood to cook our food. A piece of soap about the size of a cent was occasionally issued. Officers were put to great straits on washing-days, possessing no extra clothes an old blanket was wrapped around the person until the work was accomplished and the washed clothes dried. Daily, grotesque and laughable scenes were to be witnessed on every hand.

About the first of July, there were sixteen hundred officers in the "pen." To facilitate the issuing of the rations, the prisoners were divided into companies of one hundred, called squads; then sub-divided into twenties, called messes. One from each squad, and also from each mess, was appointed commissary. Their duties consisted in dividing and issuing properly; then there was a general commissary for all the officers in the prison, who received the rations in bulk from the rebel quartermaster.

Macon was the only prison where cooking utensils were given to us in a sufficiently large number to supply our wants. The following articles were issued to each squad of one hundred men.

    5 Iron skillets, with covers.
   15 Iron skillets, without covers.
   10 Tin pails, or buckets holding five quarts.
   10 Small tin pans, in which to mix meal.
    5 Wooden pails, or buckets.

Dull axes and miserable spades were issued each morning and returned to the gate at sundown. Any neglect to return either of them, kept all out till the missing one was returned.

The amount and kind of rations, issued each five days, was as follows:

    6 Pints of corn-meal.
    $\frac{1}{2}$ Pint of sorghum.
    $\frac{1}{8}$ Pound maggoty, rancid bacon.
    2 Table-spoonfuls of beans or rice, black and wormy.
    2 Table-spoonfuls of salt.

If necessity over the earth is appropriately called the mother of invention, in a prison we must style it the father, for some of the most useful and ingenious contrivances to live were matured and brought into existence through the talent of the captives. Knives, forks and spoons were manufactured from wood, as also dishes and soles for shoes. Rags were sewed together into passable shirts and pantaloons. Nice looking caps were made out of old cloth. Slap-jacks, out of corn-meal, were cooked on pieces of iron, so as not to stick, without grease, by the fertile brain of the Yankee captive. Not a bad substitute for coffee was brought to light out of burnt corn-meal. Vinegar was made from sorghum, and yeast from meal. Hish-hash, stews, duffs and puddings were served up occasionally, from the every day corn-meal. There was not an issue at Macon of meat but was very maggoty; after going through a Northern purrification it tasted sweet.

Sutlering was carried on extensively at this place. Prices were enormous for everything. Cashmeyer, a rebel sutler, brought in his goods in a wagon under guard, daily, and handed them over to Captain Platt, a Federal officer and prisoner, who acted for him inside of the prison, and received a share of the profits. One-third more money was asked for articles inside of the jail than outside. It was downright rascality; extortion. The poor captives only possessed a little change, who had secreted it from the rebels, and were required to pay six prices for some little delicacy. The inside sutler always lived better than his companions; but from what we have seen, the majority of officers have little respect for any Federal prisoner who acts as sutler.

In this prison the Federal officers were subjected to petty tyranny, and insulted in the grossest manner by a wretch calling himself Brady. Like Bradford, he had been a Baltimore thug, and by his sneaking, cowardly disposition had worked his way to be a factotum in a prison at the rear. A spirit of patriotism pervaded all hearts; they knew their country's strength, and power, and that its flag would one day bring freedom. They did say to their savage jailors, the boys are coming to

> "Open the prison's living tomb,
> And usher from its brooding gloom
> The victims of your savage code,
> To the free sun and air of God!"

CHAPTER X.

Preaching—Consolation of Religion—Non-Combatants—The Chaplain and Rebel General—Rebel Officers Stealing—Federal Officer "Bucked"—Rumors—Gambling—"Fresh Fish"—Amusements.

"To the sages who spoke, to the heroes who bled,
   To the day and the deed, strike the harp strings of glory!
Let the song of the ransomed remember the dead,
And the tongue of the eloquent hallow the story!
     O'er the bones of the bold
     Be the story long told,
And on fame's golden tablets their triumphs enrolled,
Who on Freedom's green hills Freedom's banner unfurled,
And the beacon-fire raised that gave light to the world!"

Although the prison hours passed slowly over our heads at Macon, there were evenings of social intercourse, pleasure and profit. Bolts and bars can never chain the mind; dungeons and starvation cannot alter the true heart's principles, or change the conscience in its obligation to God. Shackles can be placed upon the limbs, but not on the soul's worship. The thinking man will have an altar in his prison-pen, of hope, ambition, or true-God glory. Can the Christian's spirit be put in fetters, and made to offer petitions to wrong, sin, Satan and the world? No. You may scourge the flesh, immure in dark cells, reeking with filth and the tainted air poisonous, but all will only strengthen the faith of the good,—only awaken new life in the upright and holy—only bring out petitions to an Almighty Father. Rebel barbarity helped to renew devotion to country and God. Religious meetings were held on Tuesday and Saturday evenings, with benefit to the souls of all present. There were two chaplains held as prisoners, contrary to all the rules and regulations established by both governments for the exchange of non-combatants. Surgeons were also held in confinement by the rebels, contrary to agreement. But this bad faith on the part of the rebels was consistent with their every action during the war. The surgeons and chaplains remonstrated with the rebel officials concerning this dishonorable course on their part, but never could receive any satisfactory intelligence. The chaplains preached every Sabbath, nor did they ever officiate, or expound God's word to more attentive and devout listeners.

One of the chaplains related the following incident which occurred when he was taken prisoner:

I was conducted to the head-quarters of one of the commanding generals, who said to me in a half angry manner.

"Let's have a drink and play a game of cards; you pretend to be a chaplain, and as you don't do anything else, you must be good at both."

I answered to the effect:

"General, I make no pretensions; I'm a minister of the Almighty, and it is contrary to the principles of my faith to engage in any kind of games with cards, or in social intercourse to imbibe spiritous liquors. It is unjust in you to insult me in this way!"

"Chaplain, here is your Bible," said the General, holding up a pack of cards, "and here is the altar at which you worship," displaying a bottle of commissary whiskey; "I am something of a backslider from both, and if you are zealous in your religion, you can make a convert."

"General, you not only treat with contempt a minister of the gospel, but you insult a helpless captive."

"Chaplain, this bottle, and these cards, were in your saddle bags; I am convinced Yankee chaplains don't carry whiskey for food, or cards to amuse the sick. You can go on, under guard; if you are a chaplain, we don't need a devil."

The trouble was, the same day the chaplain was captured, saddles had been exchanged with the colonel. The commandant of the regiment had the chaplain's Bible and Hymn Book, whilst he had the "fighting material." The man of the Lord made explanations, but he might as well have reasoned with a block of wood as the ungodly rebel.

The Confederate officers of the day who came into the yard on duty took every opportunity to make prisoners uncomfortable. What little power they did have was meanly displayed. A petty spirit of tyranny was resorted to in the issuing of the wood and rations. A prisoner who had anything he would like to dispose of outside of the jail, could secure a rebel's service to sell it for him, but he would never receive either the money or the article. They would not only lie, but steal. Many of the prisoners lost articles through the rascality of these rebel officials. Adjutant Elkins sent a fine sash out by the officer of the day to be sold for a trifle. Whether he disposed of it for money, or appropriated it to his own use, could never be ascertained. The sneak-thief never gave an account of it. Captain Tabb, commandant of the prison, was a man who would stoop to any mean action. There was not a spark of mercy in his heart. He was a selfish, unprincipled scoundrel.

> "A mere soldier, a mere tool, a kind
> Of human sword in a fiend's hand: the other
> Is master-mover of his warlike puppet."

An officer sent out a gold watch by him to be sold. Tabb made an effort to get the officer to accept a few dollars of Confederate money, but he refused it, and demanded his watch, threatening to report him if it was not returned. Tabb then ordered him to do some menial work in front of his office; the officer refused to comply with his order. Tabb then made threats to shoot him. The officer not to be intimidated, still refused. He was then "bucked" for over two hours, suffering much pain in his cramped position.

Every day dozens of rumors were flying around

the prison, that an exchange had been agreed
upon; that the rebel officers said the Yankees had
recognized the South, and we were all to go home
in a few days; that we would be paroled and sent
through the lines immediately; that the rebels had
concluded not to take any more prisoners. This
would have been an act of mercy in comparison to
capturing and then starving them. In different
parts of the prison captives could be seen talking
excitedly over as wild and absurd stories as the
mind ever conceived. The more quiet and thinking officers would retire to the *holes* (all descriptions of rat-passages were burrowed under the buildings and in different corners; and, of course, in
rainy weather the inmates were washed out) and
become absorbed with *"exchange on the brain."*

At one time there was considerable cash at Macon, and gambling was resorted to by men who,
before their entry into prison, had never thrown
dice or fingered a card. Money changed hands
among starving and dying men; occasionally the
chaplains launched forth invectives against the un-
gentlemanly practice.

An act as disreputable in its character as gambling was practised by many on the arrival of a
new capture. All would crowd around the unfortunate, and a hundred questions be put to him at
the same time about the "news," the "army," "date
of capture," the "situation and prospect." The
older captives, who are in the outside circle,

and who cannot hear, or put questions, welcome him with cries of "Fresh fish!" "Give him air!" "Don't take his clothes!" "Take your hand out of his pocket!" "Don't put lice on him!" which creates a laugh; and it is said a laugh in prison is as good as a meal. We are sorry to say the mirth is generally at the expense of the new-comer, or "Fresh fish." If the rebels have not completely starved and stripped him, his appearance is in striking contrast with the emaciated forms, ragged garments and naked looks of those who have been so long incarcerated in Southern hells. General Schaler on his arrival at Macon was greeted with "Fresh fish," "Don't put lice on him!" Drawing himself up to his full height he reproachfully, and in a loud, firm voice, said,

"I would like to know where the Federal officers are?"

The rebuke was sufficient to disperse the crowd.

The first six months of prison-life an officer is called a *"Fresh fish;"* the next four months, *"A Sucker;"* the next two months, *"A Dry Cod;"* the balance of his time, a *"Dried Herring;"* and after exchange, a *"Pickled Sardine."*

When possible, amusements were indulged in, to pass the monotony of the weary hours. Cricket, wicket, base ball, chess and checkers, were the principal games enjoyed by the captives. There were several classes in sword exercise. The largest was taught by a little Frenchman. Officers would say:

"If we live to get out of here, and the war is over, we may still be of service to the country."

They looked to the future and thought:

>"He who maintains his country's laws
>   Alone is great; or he who dies in a good cause."

CHAPTER XI.

The Georgia Militia—Murder of Lieutenant Gierson—Plans for an Uprising—Spies—Remarkable Escapes—Captain Gibbs—Tunneling—Traitors—Fourth of July Celebration—Sherman—"Tramp, Tramp"—Lieutenant Davis.

> "Thou, too, sail on, O ship of State!
> Sail on, O Union, strong and great!
> Humanity with all its fears,
> With all the hopes of future years,
> Is hanging breathless on thy fate!
> We know what Master laid thy keel,
> What workmen wrought thy ribs of steel,
> Who made each mast, and sail, and rope,
> What anvils rang, what hammers beat,
> In what a forge and what a heat
> Were shaped the anchors of thy hope!
> Fear not each sudden sound and shock,—
> 'Tis of the wave and not the rock,
> 'Tis but the flapping of the sail,
> And not a rent made by the gale!
> In spite of rock and tempest roar,
> In spite of false lights on the shore,
> Sail on, nor fear to breast the sea!
> Our hearts, our hopes, are all with thee.
> Our hearts, our hopes, our prayers, our tears,
> Our faith triumphant o'er our fears,
> Are all with thee,—are all with thee!"

The Georgia militia guarding the Macon jail were vindictive and brutal, and their officers encouraged them in their savage acts. Promotion and furloughs were promised, and given, to those who would shoot, or kill a Yankee. All the officers were careful not to go beyond the allotted bounds, as the watchful eyes of the miscreants were always upon them. Everything was done to annoy us. Sick men, and those troubled with diarrhoea, were threatened with death if they visited the sink at night. The most savage people never surpassed the rebels in the treatment of sick foes. They would sing, shout, dance and call the hours from sun-set to sun-rise. They contrived the most diabolical schemes to allow us no rest night nor day. They would have three or four roll-calls through the day, and their carnivals at night. On the 11th of June Lieutenant Gierson, of the Fifty-ninth New York, an inoffensive, gallant soldier, was murdered within ten feet of the "dead-line." He was shot by Richard Barrett, of the twenty-seventh Georgia Battalion. The murderer received a corporal's stripes, and I think a furlough, for his *Southern* bravery, in sending an unarmed, helpless captive into eternity. If the Government does not, or cannot, seek out these devils, it is consoling to know that there is a righteous God who will not allow the guilty to escape.

In this prison there were several organizations, or clubs, started for the purpose of breaking out of the "pen." A strong guard came in to attend roll-call, and it was believed they carried a sufficient number of arms with which to effect our liberty. Some of the most meritorious and gallant officers in the United States army were confined here. They favored the plan, if we accomplished our freedom, to repair to Andersonville, fifty or sixty miles distant, and release the thirty thousand starving and naked men confined there, and with this poorly provisioned, but heroic host, "break things up generally" in the Confederacy. The scheme was a bold but feasible one. Whether there was a traitor in camp, or the suspicions of the rebels were aroused, the large guard ceased coming into the yard about the time the attempt was to be made.

Hounds were kept near the jail, to put on the track of any ingenious prisoner who succeeded in getting outside the "pen!" There was a small run ran through a corner of the stockade, used for the sink, and out of this unclean opening an officer made his escape; and though the country was alarmed, and the hounds put on the scent, the bold, fearless and inventive genius reached our lines. Many others succeeded in getting out of the prison. Their troubles and trials only commenced then. They were brought back, some of them having travelled hundreds of miles, and were caught in the act of going through the lines.

Occasionally a colored man would come into the prison to do some menial service. An officer profited by this fact, blackened himself with burnt wood and passed out of the gate, and through a a number of guards, but unfortunately the poor fellow was caught after leaving town.

Lieutenant Wilson went out in a small box, on

the sutler wagon, through the agency of "Black Charley," the driver, when two rebels were guarding it closely. He was brought back. All honor to the loyal black man! He deserves the thanks of every lover of his country, as he risked his life for a Union captive.

One day a workman came into the stockade to repair the pumps. An officer dressed in gray pantaloons and an old jacket, secured his pick-axe, put on a bold face, went to the gate, said he had his work done, passed by the guards and commanding officer, out into the country. I am sorry to say, this smart and gallant officer was recaptured after travelling one hundred miles.

Captain Gibbs, who relieved Tabb, was a low-spirited, designing knave. He was one of those malicious rascals, who cared not on which side he took part, providing there were no risks and dangers to be incurred, and his bread was well buttered. He not only fleeced the prisoners, but cheated the rebels. He was continually "feathering his nest," for the day of sorrow, when the bottom of the Confederacy would fall out. For some spite he had a Federal officer taken out of the "pen," and accused of deserting from the Rebel army. After undergoing many privations and sufferings, through the influence of this vagabond, he was returned to the prison with a broken-down constitution.

All the officers at Macon took an interest in the sanitary condition of our prison. As it was the warm season every care was taken to prevent disease. The rebels made pretensions to clean the camp, but had not the officers done the "policing," a plague would have carried off all of us. But few died during the two months I was here.

Some fifty general and field officers were sent to Charleston, it was reported, for exchange, which caused some excitement. They were sent to be placed under fire, without cause or provocation, which was one of the most barbarous acts, committed by a people in war, during modern times. It was Southern chivalry!

Tunneling operations were carried on extensively at Macon. There were as many as six in progress at one time. The plan of carrying on the work was in the following manner: A retired spot, perhaps under a bunk, was selected as close by the "dead-line" as possible; then dig down three or four feet, about two feet from the top strike horizontally towards the outside of the stockade, the opening being about large enough for a man to work in lying down. During the day a board was placed in the hole, one foot or so from the top, then filled up with dirt, carefully tramped down, and swept over, so that all traces of the digging might be effaced. To carry on business systematically, a company was formed. One would be placed on guard, another would enter the hole and dig, whilst a third would haul the dirt to the mouth of the hole, in a bag or box fastened to a string, and a fourth party carried it off in kettles or haversacks to the sink, or under the building, or scattered it through the yard, to be cleaned up on the morrow, and carried out in the police cart. Of course when finished it opened on the outside of the "pen," and on the appointed night, the underground track would be taken for liberty. It was fatiguing, hard labor, smothering work in warm weather. I remember hauling one poor fellow out of the hole suffocated. Several times those effecting the narrow path to liberty have fainted. It was also slow work, as an erect position could not be obtained for digging. All the work had to be done lying on the stomach, and with an old knife, or some very poor tool. In sultry weather reliefs were sent in every fifteen minutes. It generally took from three to four weeks to complete one. On the 27th of June, 1864, three were discovered or pointed out by a traitor,—two were finished, and to be used that night. There was much excitement in consequence of this detection. Interrogatories would be put to each other, "Who told the rebels?" "How did they find it out?" "If we only knew the man we would hang him!" some passionate captive would cry. The guilty party was suspected, never discovered. He did not come to his home in the North; he is buried at Columbia, South Carolina.

There was a great mania for maps of the country when the tunneling was under way. All wanted to know how and where to go in case a path was opened for freedom. School-boy memories of States and rivers, bridges, swamps and mountains were brought to remembrance. The man whose geography was good, generally had a crowd around him; for both parties this was unfortunate if they crowded together at night, for the guard had orders to fire at any small group.

One of the happiest days I ever spent in prison was the 4th of July, 1864. A day long to be remembered by every heart, an occasion that will be recalled by those present, with feelings of pride and pleasure. After roll-call, when the count was made, and the officers were standing in groups around the prison yard, a Captain Todd, a very tall man, of the 8th New Jersey Volunteers, placed in his hat a small silk flag, four by six inches, which had been presented to him by a lady of Jersey City, and which he had up to this time kept secreted from the rebels. No sooner was the banner displayed than it was welcomed with three hearty cheers, which said, "We still love our country; there are no traitors here." An officer struck up the "Star Spangled Banner," which was sung in a fine, manly voice, with artistic taste, every one present joining in the chorus, with the full power of the lungs.

O! say, can you see, by the dawn's early light,
 What so proudly we hail'd at the twilight's last gleaming;
Whose broad stripes and bright stars, through the perilous fight,
 O'er the ramparts we watched were so gallantly streaming?
And the rocket's red glare, the bombs bursting in air,
 Gave proof through the night that our flag was still there.
O! say, does the Star spangled banner still wave
 O'er the land of the free and the home of the brave?

All by mutual consent proceeded to the large building in the centre of the prison, when Chaplain Dixon, 16th Connecticut Volunteers, made a most appropriate, patriotic and feeling prayer. Speeches were made by Captains Ives, Lee and Kellogg, Lieutenant Ogden, Chaplains Whitney and Dixon, interspersed with patriotic songs, recitations of poetry breathing a love of freedom and country. "Sweet Home" was sung, which brought tears to every eye present. Over all our heads floated the emblem of freedom, the stars and stripes, the flag of our country. All, as they gazed on its little stars and stripes, renewed their love and devotion to the cause of humanity, country and the crushing of the rebellion. All of us had felt the blood-thirsty tyranny of Southern slave-dealers and the grinding heel of an unmerciful foe, and appreciated the blessings, privileges and value of just laws and good government, and pledged again, although surrounded by rebel bayonets, our lives in sustaining our country's constitution and honor, and blotting out every traitor in the land. Colonel Thorp was delivering a most eloquent and noble address, full of patriotism, counsel and encouragement, when a rebel officer appeared in our midst with an order breaking up the meeting. Our celebration was over; we could not thus meet, even in prison, to speak words of cheer and kindness to each other. The crowd noiselessly went to their quarters, comforted, and feeling it was one of the happiest and most glorious fourths of July ever they had spent.

In the afternoon an order appeared on the "Bulletin Board," inside the jail, to the folllowing effect.

[SPECIAL ORDER NO. 6.]
C. S. MILITARY PRISON, MACON, GA.,
July 4th, 1864.

I. Lieutenant-Colonel Thorp is relieved from duty as Senior Officer of Prisons, for a violation of prison rules, and Lieutenant-Colonel McCrary will again assume that position.

II. The same order and quiet will be observed on this day as any other.

III. A disregard to this order may subject offenders to unpleasant consequences.

GEORGE C. GIBBS,
Captain Commanding.

My readers can judge what the rebels mean when they say "unpleasant consequences." Notwithstanding this order, some Yankee genius had a display of fire-works at night.

For weeks after the anniversary could be heard ringing in our ears:

> Yes, we'll rally round the flag, boys, we'll rally once again,
> Shouting the battle cry of Freedom;
> We will rally from the hill-side, we'll gather from the plain,
> Shouting the battle cry of Freedom.
>
> > The Union forever, hurrah, boys, hurrah!
> > Down with the traitor, up with the star;
> > While we rally round the flag, boys, rally once again,
> > Shouting the battle cry of Freedom.

We are springing to the call for Three Hundred Thousand more,
  Shouting the battle cry of Freedom;
And we'll fill the vacant ranks of our brothers gone before,
  Shouting the battle cry of Freedom.

    The Union forever, hurrah, boys, hurrah!
    Down with the traitor, up with the star;
    While we rally round the flag, boys, rally once again,
    Shouting the battle cry of Freedom.

We will welcome to our numbers the loyal, true, and brave,
  Shouting the battle cry of Freedom;
And although he may be poor he shall never be a slave,
  Shouting the battle cry of Freedom.

    The Union forever, hurrah, boys, hurrah!
    Down with the traitor, up with the star;
    While we rally round the flag, boys, rally once again,
    Shouting the battle cry of Freedom.

So we're springing to the call from the East and from the West,
  Shouting the battle cry of Freedom;
And we'll hurl the rebel crew from the land we love the best,
  Shouting the battle cry of Freedom.

    The Union forever, hurrah, boys, hurrah!
    Down with the traitor, up with the star;
    While we rally round the flag, boys, rally once again,
    Shouting the battle cry of Freedom.

We had rumors every day of our removal to Charleston, or some safe place. Sherman was marching where he pleased: he was before Atlanta; his troopers were every place. At night we could hear his cannon thundering. All was bustle and excitement outside of the prison; stock was coming into Macon; trains were running night and day; the rebels became frightened, and we said:

    "Tramp, tramp, tramp, the boys are marching,
      Cheer up, comrades, they will come."

It became evident if we were not moved soon,

our forces would rescue us. Hope and life took possession of the prison. Officers took their customary exercises, chatting, playing, walking up and down. Colonel Brown, a humorous man, full of life, always singing, had been sent to Charleston under fire, and for a time there was gloom and despondency in the jail; but Sherman's cannon awakened animation and joy again. On Sabbath evening the secesh ladies would gaze on us from a platform, with neither feelings of love nor pity. In Macon they would talk of visiting the "show," to see the live Yankees. They saw more than any lady would wish to see.

Lieutenant Davis had charge of the prison latterly. His appearance caused mirth; he had a long feather stuck in his hat; dressed like an Italian robber; he looked as if he was "got up" for the stage. He would strut around night and day seeking tunnels. Some officers said he was crazy,—others, if he was not, he soon would be.

> ' He raves, his words are loose
> As heaps of sand, and scattering wide from sense:
> So high he's mounted on his airy throne,
> That now the wind has got into his head,
> And turns his brain to phrenzy."

CHAPTER XII.

Savannah Prison—Nearly Recaptured—Incident on Route—A Southern Mother Fooled—Our Parade in Savannah—Secesh Females—Our Quarters—Food and Water—The Sutler—Cow Falls into a Tunnel—A Federal Officer Becomes Crazy—Escapes—Hardships.

> "O Prison! how shall I thee avoid? or with what spell
> Dissolve the enchantment of thy magic cell?
> Ev'n *Fox* himself can't boast so many martyrs,
> As yearly fall within thy wretched quarters.
> Money I've none, and debts I cannot pay,
> Unless my vermin will those debts defray.
> Not scolding wife, nor inquisition's worse;
> Thou'rt ev'ry mischief cramm'd into one curse."

In the latter part of July, 1864, an order came for our removal. Six hundred were started for Charleston. Two or three days afterwards the second six hundred, with the writer in company, were placed in the close box-cars, under a heavy guard, and took their departure for Savannah. As our forces were closing in on the Confederacy, and driving them to its center, it became a difficult matter to guard the prisoners. They did not look to our welfare or comfort; the death of a captive gave them pleasure; their great object was to keep us. Our cavalry came very nearly releasing us and destroying the train a short distance from Macon. Fifteen minutes after leaving the station where we stopped for wood and water, the troopers destroyed the telegraph office, rolling stock, public buildings, and tore up the track for hundreds of yards, creating the greatest alarm and excitement throughout that section of country. In the afternoon we heard the news, and there was sadness in every heart, when we reflected how near we had been to our forces and liberty.

We had received orders not to take our cooking utensils with us; but many of the boys smuggled buckets kettles and skillets through to Savannah. And it was fortunate they did, for it was several days before these necessary articles were issued; then not in sufficient numbers to supply our wants. I had put on my shoes for the first time since I entered the Macon prison, and few would believe the strange sensation felt in walking. I wore the soles of my shoes as thin as paper, in the journey over the country, when I tried to escape from the rebels; and looking at the future, not knowing where the next would come from, and if I were alive and not exchaged in the winter, I would suffer from the frost, I went barefoot in the summer. It was fortunate I did so, for, bad as they were, they prevented many a cold, and saved hours of suffering, tramping the frosty ground.

At one of the way stations a Southern woman took me for a rebel and I was treated with remarkable kindness. She discovered her error before the train started. I had talked a guard into accompanying me to procure some water at a well, in a farm yard, alongside of the railroad. She said in Georgia hish-hash.

"So yees been catching more Yankees? O, the ablition niggers; I'se got two youngsters with Lee and Milledge is gone the week after Sunday; watch 'em, blow 'em, kill 'em if theys says yellow."

This was spoken to me, as she took me for a rebel soldier; and as far as it concerned dress, I looked like one, having on an old pair of confederacy pantaloons, a white patched hat, and a ragged coat of all colors. I said:

"Yes, my good woman, the Yankees are tricky; we'll take care of them. Can't you let us have some bread?"

"I'as'nt been to the mill for a time, and I's short, but yees can have a dodger."

As soon as I had got the food in my possession; and was out of the gate, I shouted:

"You are sold this time, old lady. I fight for Lincoln. Hurrah for the Union!"

The Southern mother looked frightened and uttered a language which was far from lady-like, as I jumped on the car, clutching my dodger, and rode off.

At this station an officer came very near losing his life. He had received permission from a guard to get off the car a few minutes. His feet scarcely touched the ground when a ruffian from the top fired at him. Fortunately the ball passed through his hat. God pointed the gun!

We arrived in the city of Savannah about sundown, and were formed in line on the street, gazed upon by a motley crowd of all ages and sexes, perhaps the largest number of people ever assembled at one place, having neither love nor pity in their hearts. After parading the principal streets, making a better appearance and behaving superior to our guards, we were confined in part of the yard belonging to the U. S. Marine Barracks. It embraced a few acres of level, sandy ground. Some of the most violent secession women in the South are to be found in Savannah. Women are supposed to breathe a spirit of pity, moderation and forbearance; to display feelings of magnanimity and mercy towards mankind, when they possess influence. In all ages and all countries the tender sex have been the first to shed tears of pity for friend or foe, and the last to forsake in time of need, or when danger threatened. Women in Savannah, we will not say all, lost sight of this heavenly disposition and feeling, and in a shameful manner insulted the poor, sick, unarmed, hungry, and badly clothed prisoners of war. It was an outrage on the sex. One said:

"How do yees like the corn-dodger?" Yees 'ill get used to it ere yees go North."

Another, leaning out of a parlor window, called her boy to her and said,

"Shake this little Southern flag in the Yankees' faces."

Others sung, or rather shouted, the "Bonny Blue Flag," and "Dixie," whilst the rabble cheered, shouted, hissed and bellowed like *calves.*

Two or three officers made their escape from the cars between Macon and Savannah. One young man, a gun-boat officer, jumped off and ran into the woods; although five or six shots were fired at him, none took effect. He was afterwards recaptured, put in irons, and maltreated in a brutal manner.

A high stockade of boards was erected between the prison camp and Barrack's building. Six hundred of us were alotted about one-third of the yard; a small space to crowd so many into. A brick wall six feet high surrounded the prison on three sides. There were six feet of stockade added to the wall, and two or three sentry boxes on each side of the pen, erected after the style of the Macon prison, so the guards could see all that took place within the enclosure. There were a few shade trees on the north-west side of the camp. The "dead-line" was similar to that at Macon. The fires, which were lit at night, were raised four feet from the ground. A detail was made which kept these fires burning all night. Common little "A" tents were issued, at the rate of one for six or seven men. These were arranged in streets, and many of them raised from the ground two or three feet, with bunks in. One pump for a long time supplied the prison with water. This water became very bad; its smell and taste was like that obtained at the Sulphur Springs in Virginia. Finally but few would drink it; carrion and decayed meat being pumped up daily. Several of the messes by a process of filtering purified and rendered the water healthy. A hydrant was introduced which supplied us with plenty of river water which was muddy and very bad. We were supplied with cooking utensils; and also received the best supply of food ever issued at rebel prisons. Several of the squads had nice ovens, built with brick and lime. Savannah was the only place we got fresh meat, and any kind of decent treatment, although many of the men who had been brought from Andersonville suffered from exposure, bad usage and want of food, at a prison some squares from the Marine Barracks.

One day a working party of black people came into the yard, composed of seven *women*, and as many boys. The work was the covering of our *sink*. The rebels looked upon the women as animals, nor did they care to what base uses they put them. Among the party was a *white* boy; none of the prisoners would believe he was a negro, but the rebel officer said:

"He's a nigger and a *slave!*"

At this prison much anger was manifested towards the sutler, who charged a dozen prices for his articles. One of our officers, inside the prison, acted as his agent, and received a share of abuse. Not satisfied with a sufficient amount to live on, he attempted extortion; saved money and sought to buy greenbacks; not for the rebels, but *himself.* How mean?

Tunneling and mining operations were conducted with spirit during the first month's captivity at Savannah. Fortune did not seem to favor these underground tracks to Freedom. As I resolved to make another attempt for escape, I entered with earnestness into all the work of these narrow paths to liberty. A splendid tunnel was completed, which ran from a tent through an old well, under the foundation of the wall, into the street. The lack of air and breathing was so difficult in the construction of this "hole" that a fan, or bellows, had to be manufactured, and placed at the mouth of the avenue, to give air to the worker, to enable him to proceed with his business. Once I was hauled from the hole more dead than alive. When we reached the well, it was discovered to be a a good place to secrete the dirt which would come from the unfinished tunnel. The very night it was to be opened, a cow fell through it, which led to its discovery. The rebels did not say anything, but placed a guard at its mouth, on the outside. The first man who was to "lead off" in going out caught a glimpse of the sentinel, and beat a retreat inside of the prison. All was discovered; our work was vain; but fortunately no lives were lost. All is for the best. If I had got out that night I would have attempted to swim the Savannah river, a wide, swift stream, and would perhaps have gone to the bottom. The rebels now watched us closely and looked for tunnels every day. The rebel soldiers who kept the fires going at night looked in every tent. They would put their heads inside of the officers' quarters and ask some foolish question to cover their design, such as: "Do you want to buy a shirt?" "Have you any buttons for sale?" They discovered several in progress of construction. They would also steal what they could lay their hands on. Several officers lost hats, shoes, coats, etc. One officer had a watch stolen, but recovered it through the exertions of Colonel Wayne, the rebel commandant. Although Wayne was crabbed and ill-natured, and approached the savage in his nature and disposition, he was strictly honest. He had a peculiar way of insulting prisoners. We felt honored with his orders, though their style was evidently intended to taunt us. The following is similar to one of his orders:

{ HEAD-QUARTERS,
{ CAMP OF YANKEE PRISONERS.
August 28*th*, 1864.

[*Special Orders, No.* 3.]

I. The tent will be taken from the "*Yankees*," prisoners, in which a "mining operation" is discovered.

II. The inmates will be handed over to the Provost Marshall for *close* confinement.

——— Wayne,
Lieutenant-Colonel Commanding.

Two officers were taken out of the "pen," and confined in a damp, unhealthy cell. They were allowed little food and abused in a shameful manner, *for attempting to escape!*

Major Hill who came into the prison occasionally treated us decently, as "prisoners of war." He did all that lay in his power to obtain a valuable ring for one of the sick prisoners, which was kept by one of the rebels who had taken it out to sell. He bought some reading matter for one of the squads that had collected some Confederate money. The books helped to while away many a weary hour. Many are indebted to Lieutenant Ogden, a Federal officer, for his instructions in grammar and the sciences.

At this prison an officer, Lieutenant Burroughs, or Burrows, became completely crazy from the effects of "prison life." Daily he was to be seen walking with straws and feathers in his head and hat; making steam engines with chips; talking to himself about inventions; with a rod and string fishing in the water trough. It was a sad, sorrowful sight! Officers were continually watching him that he should not go to the "dead-line" and lose his life.

One evening a guard, watching his opportunity, threw me a newspaper. He was a Union man. Orders against this were very strict, and the act was done perhaps at the risk of his life.

The chaplains left this prison for exchange.

One preached a farewell sermon. There were few dry eyes in the assembly. At the close of the services, by the request of the chaplain, the audience raised their right hands to heaven, and pledged themselves to a life of usefulness and to God. Whilst with us, every Sabbath they held divine service. At this time there was much talk about exchange. All had it "on the brain."

The officers passed much of their time singing, playing ball and games, and in social amusements.

From this prison there was no successful escape made to our lines. An officer attired in rebel clothing passed out at the gate, and by the guards, but was afterwards recaptured and punished for it. Next day all the prisoners' effects were overturned by the rebels hunting grey uniforms. A bold young artillery officer, during a thunder-storm one night, jumped the "dead-line" and with a case-knife dug a hole under the stockade, near the Barracks' building, and made his escape to the swamps. The poor fellow, after undergoing many hardships and adventures by "flood and field," was recaptured and again placed in our prison, the skeleton of what he once was, from the effects of the superhuman fatigues he had undergone.

> "Sweet are the uses of adversity;
> Which, like the toad, ugly and venomous,
> Wears yet a precious jewel in his head;
> And this our life, exempt from public haunt,
> Finds tongues in trees, books in running brooks,
> Sermons in stones, and good in everything."

CHAPTER XIII.

Southern Feeling—Charleston the Cradle of Rebellion—Under Fire—Jail Yard—No Food or Quarters—Fires—Shelling the City—Barbarity on Colored Soldiers—Convicts—The Cowardly Leader.

> "Drive me, O drive me from that traitor, man!
> So I might 'scape that monster, let me dwell
> In lion's haunts, or in some tiger's den;
> Place me on some steep, craggy, ruin'd rock,
> That bellies out, just dropping in the ocean;
> Bury me in the hollow of its womb:
> Where, starving on my cold and flinty bed,
> I may from far, with giddy apprehension,
> See infinite fathoms down the rumbling deep;
> Yet not e'n there, in that vast whirl of death,
> Can there be found so terrible a ruin
> As man! false man! smiling, destructive man!"

We do not know what opinions and ideas the majority of the thinking people of the South held when the rebel government ordered General Samuel Jones to place the Union officers, prisoners, under fire of their own guns. But we are forced to believe the same spirit sanctioned the act that decked the ruffians with flowers who helped to butcher our wounded in Sudley Church, after the first battle of Manassas. In Missouri the rebels took scalps as trophies, and *ladies* who boasted of their refinement decorated their parlors with these ghastly mementoes of cruelty. Though seeming incredible, it is true, that personal ornaments were made from the bones of our unburied dead, and that Southern women wore them. It has been proved beyond question. The civilized world is acquainted with the fact that sixty thousand of our poor prisoners were literally starved in a country where Sherman's army of one hundred thousand men found supplies so abundant that they could dispense with their wagon train. No act was too cowardly, base, and blood-thirsty for the first-families, the slave-holders of the South. The *ladies* and *gentlemen* who endorsed these acts, and smiled on the men who murdered our surrendered soldiers at Fort Pillow, surely encouraged and gave their assent to the placing of our men under fire at Charleston. According to all the rules and regulations governing civilized nations in time of war, an enemy has no right to hold captives they cannot quarter and feed, and treat in every respect as "prisoners of war." It is said we were placed in Charleston on account of the scarcity of provisions in other portions of the land, and partly as security against Federal raiding parties We know that they could not have held us in Georgia, but in Charleston there was a greater scarcity of provisions than in any other portion of the country held by the rebels. Most of the food arriving at Charleston came from the interior of South Carolina. It is a base falsehood that we were placed in Charleston on account of the lack of food in other parts. Then why was it we were confined in the lower part of the city, where our shells fell thickest? Away with Southern lying and subterfuge! The Federal gunners operating against Charleston knew our places of confinement, and being expert in their science, threw shells every place but where we were imprisoned. Were there no other places close by Charleston out of range of our guns? None of our men suffered from Federal shells, but an ever-watchful Almighty surrounded them with His arms, and protected them from brutal foes practising their refined cruelty. God pointed the guns, and the swift messengers sped, not to take away Union life, but to shatter and shock depraved rebel hearts.

On September 13th, we were taken from the prison-pen, and shut up in the loathsome box-cars, and taken to Charleston. Orders had been given not to take the cooking utensils along, but fortunately many of the boys smuggled kettles and skillets through the journey. We were placed in the City Jail Yard, one of the uncleanest spots in the whole South. Six hundred of us were crowded into a small, filthy space, scarcely one acre. A brick wall, twelve feet high, surrounded the yard, whilst the jail building stood near the northern center. The jail though out of repair was a splendid, commanding piece of workmanship. A dilapidated and frightful looking gallows occupied a position at one end of the yard. There were a few old tents in the prison, enough to give quarters to one hundred and twenty-five, allowing four and six in a tent; consequently there were over four hundred who did not have any kind of shelter to protect from a drizzling rain, or the scorching, burning heat of a Southern sun. Those who occupied tents were flooded out in wet weather. A cistern supplied us with a little rain-water; but when it rained, all the dirt and filth of the yard ran into the cistern, as its mouth was level with the ground, so that the very time we should have had plenty of water, if arrangements had been made for our comfort, we did not have any fit for use. There was an artesian well that supplied us with very poor brackish water. For the first two days after our entrance into the jail we received neither rations nor wood. Many of the officers were weak from hunger, and actually starving. The rations issued were the uncleanest we got at any prison. A few small kettles were issued for us to cook in, but no skillets or pans. With most of the officers mush was the principal diet; dry, unpalatable mush, that gave neither health nor strength. Two meals a day, mush for dinner, and warmed up, if we were fortunate to have enough wood, for supper. At the prison jail there was not one mess that had sufficient cooking utensils to supply eight men. Skillets and kettles were constantly in use. Every one was borrowing. Nearly all the cooking utensils in the yard had been smuggled from the Savannah "pen." It was fortunate such was the case, for much starvation and suffering was thus alleviated. At one time there was not a stick of wood issued for four days, and there were officers in the yard who had not tasted food for forty-eight hours, and were then forced to eat raw meal to sustain life.

On our arrival in the "cradle of secession" many of the chivalric sons and daughters of the boastful city turned out to see us; but they did not look upon us with friendly eyes. Their spirits were broken. They were not as proud and haughty as when sixty thousand men attacked a handful of brave soldiers in Fort Sumpter. They had felt the effects of the war, and the scales were falling from their eyes, and they began to see the folly and wickedness of their doings. They had more respect for Northern people and institutions now than formerly. They were fast realizing the strength and majesty of the government they had spit upon and set at defiance. The only persons who manifested sympathy and looked upon us with friendly feelings were the colored people. We knew their hearts were with us, though they stood at a distance and rebel bayonets prevented, but did not control, demonstations in favor of "Massa Lincum's gob'rnment." Several Irish women eluded the guards and showed their love for the old flag by giving to its defenders a supply of bread and meat, at the risk of their liberty, and perhaps lives. These women were poor. One said, "Arrah, when are yees comin to relave us; if yees don't come soon, ivery one of us 'ill be murthered?"

Early one morning there was considerable excitement in the prison. A colored boy who had been abused by one of the guards, laughed at him, when the guard took the strap of his gun and beat him shamefully. The boy told the ruffian that there was a good time coming, when the rebel raised his rifle and shot him dead. The guard was not punished, nor even relieved, but continued on duty at his post.

A good many officers of Sherman's army left this jail for exchange. Between the rebels and several confined here there was much foul play and bribery to effect a release. Several officers who should have gone, were compelled to remain behind, owing to a want of honor on the part of the rebels.

One night during a severe storm I slept in a cell in the jail. I said I slept; but I did not. I stood up all night to preserve my life from the fury of an army of bugs.

About September 19th a fire broke out in the city near the prison, and our forces threw shells in every few seconds, every one seeming to drop in the middle of the conflagration. There was continual shouting and yelling, and the whole city appeared to be wild and excited. It was thought one time the fire would reach our prison. Around our jail fell the ponderous shells of the Union guns, knocking whole houses down, bursting and tearing up everything for twenty yards, creating alarm and fear among old and young, black and white. But through God's good pleasure not a shell fell into the small place where we were all huddled together. If one had bursted in the yard, there would have been great destruction of life and limb. But a kind Almighty averted this terrible affliction. A piece of one of the deadly missiles fell into the prison, but did no damage; the only person frightened was a rebel sentinel, who dropped his rifle and skedaddled. Close by the jail was a large building called the Workhouse, in which a large number of the officers were confined. Hundreds of the officers were also held in the Marine and Roper Hospitals, large buildings contiguous to the jail. One day a shell struck the Roper Hospital and knocked things around pretty freely and *only* wounded several of our officers. It was the pleasure of a wise Providence that none of us should die by our own shells.

Confined in different cells in the jail building were a large number of colored soldiers, mostly from Massachusets, captured at the assault on Fort Wagner, in 1863, and at different times on the islands around Charleston. The Almighty only knows what these poor, brave boys endured. Many of them lacked an arm or leg. They were compelled to do all kinds of drudgery and dirty work. They never received any food but bread and wa-

I

ter. Their life was a severe burden. Many of them could read and write and were quite intelligent. One of them showed me his back, which was lacerated and hacked in a terrible manner; large, deep furrows were cut into the flesh across the shoulders and down the middle of the back. It seemed he had been flogged with some kind of a sharp instrument, heavy rods or thick rope. Several of them were excellent singers; occasionally a crowd of officers would gather beneath their cell windows and listen to their music. They had composed several patriotic songs. One was a parody on "Dearest Love, Do You Remember." The chorus was sung with great effect and pathos, and ran thus:

> "Yes, now I'm sad and lonely;
> O, how bad I feel;
> Down in Charleston, South Carolina,
> Praying for a good square meal!"

To add to our wretchedness, convicts, thieves, pickpockets, and murderers were turned out of their cells into the yard to keep our society. These bad characters, corrupt with disease and filth, ran around in our midst seeking something to steal. They did not succeed; we had nothing.

A rebel surgeon who occasionally came into the prison once said, "The sick can go to ——; I can't, and will not do anything for them." I am real sorry I could not obtain his name.

Several of our sick and emaciated boys from Andersonville, who were unable to go out to the Florence "pen," were put in the jail yard. They had neither medicine nor food. One of the poor fellows died; none would live to see home. They were skeletons, and unable to stand on their feet; nothing remained of the men but skin and bones. O humanity, humanity! But the rebels gloried in their brutality.

In the first six hundred officers who left Macon for Charleston there was an organized society to take possession of the train, and blow the engine up and smash the cars and effect an escape. The plot was to be carried into effect at the crossing of the road that ran down to Port Royal Ferry, some twenty miles from our lines, about a night's march. The guards were to have been taken along, and the picket-post captured. The colonel's heart failed him, at the proper time, when he should have given the signal with a small lamp. Had there not been a *coward* for a leader, this bold stroke for liberty would have been a success. None of the officers afterwards associated with the poltroon.

Some of the weary, tortuous time was passed in the terrible jail yard listening to a funny genius, Lieutenant Vance, sing his own songs. One was "*Louder on Exchange*," and elicited clapping of hands and shouts. Another of his songs was "*Down in Macon.*"

CHAPTER XIV.

Take a Parole to Live—Power of Attorney—Selfishness—Yellow Fever—Sisters of Charity—Vagabonds—The Silent City—Fires—Escapes—Hardee—A True Lady—Mercy.

> "A prison is in all things like a grave,
> Where we no better privileges have
> Than dead men; nor so good. The soul once fled
> Lives freer now, than when she was cloist'red
> In walls of flesh."

It was evident to every prisoner confined in the filthy jail yard that a few more weeks' suffering and misery would culminate in disease and death. Our cruel keepers, not to alleviate our terrible condition nor add to our comfort, but to relieve a portion of the guard doing duty at the jail, paroled a squad of one hundred. I was among the number. We were taken to a large private house on Broad Street, near what is called the Public Landing, in the burnt district, and fronting the Ashley River. Two guards paced their beats near the building, to prevent citizens from interfering or having intercourse with us. There was no "dead-line" here, or malicious, taunting jailors. The officers took the parole to save their lives. Had they received treatment that belongs to prisoners of war, it never would have been taken. It always had been the policy of the officers to keep a large guard around us. Every man was wanted in the rebel army, and in the paroling of us they were on hand to reenforce a threatened point. A parole will not be taken by an officer, unless his guards are withdrawn and he receives usage accorded to prisoners by civilized nations. It requires two parties to make a contract, the honor of both is concerned in its fulfillment. Though we were still under fire, we had good quarters, better food, and ragamuffins no longer pointed loaded muskets at our hearts. We were allowed the privilege of crossing the street and taking a bath in salt water, a luxury we all enjoyed. We could keep clean from vermin and filth. The pure air and bracing atmosphere renewed life and hope. Sinking and emaciated forms received strength and vigor. True, we were still captives. One day we did not receive our food here, and the rebels said it was our own fault; that one of our shells had knocked the subsistence department to pieces, and killed the commissary sergeant and those assisting in getting our rations. This was consoling to us; but our reflections were, that if a commissary sergeant was killed daily, we would not live long.

We remained at this place one week. It was the happiest week spent whilst in rebel hands. We were still prisoners, and

> "I only mark'd the glorious sun and sky,
> Too bright—too blue—for my captivity;
> And felt that all which freedom's bosom cheers
> Must break my chain before it dried my tears."

At the Broad Street building a man presented himself and offered money at the rate of two Confederate for one greenback, to any officer who would furnish him with the power of an attorney for the amount, on some responsible person North. Many accepted his offer. I took fifty dollars worth of the trash. The speculator was keen and shrewd, and he knew the Southern Confederacy would soon explode and leave him penniless, if he did not have some of Uncle Sam's money. I now bought some extras and began to look ahead, and take things in a philosophical light. My lot was truly bad, but it might be worse. I was in rags; my clothes were completely gone, and it was only by ingenuity, good care, and continual watching I was enabled to hide my nakedness. All the prisoners were in the same fix. There was no prospect of receiving clothing from home. If it was sent and came into rebel hands, they would appropriate it to their own use. I purchased needles and thread and began sewing and patching. I bought a shirt for thirty dollars that would cost about twenty cents in Philadelphia. Some bread and delicacies were bought for the mess, and again all felt tolerably happy, thought of home and wished for life. Captain Parker, of my regiment, who had secreted some money from the rebels when captured, was in my mess, and a more liberal, generous, good-hearted man never lived. There was nothing selfish in his nature. Whilst he had money it was freely appropriated for the benefit of all. There is no place like a prison for the bringing out of a person's true character. If a prisoner is stingy, narrow-minded, mean and selfish, he cannot hide it one week after confinement. Though he may have some money and possess some extra clothing, he would miserly return to his own lines rather than share, in time of trial, his store with starving and almost naked companions. The noble, whole-souled man, if he has two shirts, will part with one; if he is the owner of a dollar, he will give it to a sickly friend, or a mess-mate, to buy bread or tobacco. Every officer confined in prison recognizes both characters daily. They are well known.

About the 1st of October all the naval prisoners held by the rebels were exchanged by way of Richmond. Over one hundred navy officers left Charleston, rejoicing in the thought of a speedy release from rebel tyranny. About this time "exchange stock" ran very high. Groups of men were to be seen discussing the policy of the Rebel and Federal authorities in keeping prisoners. No complaints were heard. Savage usage and long imprisonment but fanned the flame of patriotism and love of country in the bosoms of all.

At the time so many officers were imprisoned in Charleston that terrible scourge the yellow fever broke out in the city. This fever is essentially a disease of hot climates. In some of the cities of the tropics it is rarely or never absent. In higher latitudes, as in New Orleans, Mobile and Charleston, it is frequently present, but does not prevail, as a matter of course, every summer. In the North it is only an occasional visitant, but always epidemic. This frightful devastator of communities made its appearance in a city where there were sixteen hundred Northern men confined and huddled together in small apartments, with no ventilation or sanitary regulations. All became uneasy. But was it remarkable that men from the far off North, unacclimated, and receiving poor food and poorer treatment, with no medical attendance, should feel *uneasy* when a merciless pestilence broke out in their midst? The Sisters of Charity visited our prison on Broad Street, and brought the most deplorable accounts of its ravages in the city, and among our men confined in a camp some distance out of town. The disease had broken out among them and was carrying them off in scores; the most terrible suffering prevailed; the camp was loathsome from the effects of bodies, a complete mass of corruption, being allowed to remain in the prison unburied. The Sisters brought us some tobacco and manifested a disposition to alleviate our sufferings. They had plenty of Confederate money and gave the highest price for greenbacks. One of the guards doing duty across the street took the fever and died. Next morning a corporal was carried off, and in the evening the subordinate commandant of prisons in Charleston, Captain Sheldon, died of the scourge. The city truly seemed to be a Sodom and Gomorrah. The only event that gladdened the hearts of the rebel citizens was the arrival of a blockade runner. It gave joy and inspired confidence. Occasionally about dusk on a cloudy night, from our prison, could be seen the dark-colored blockade runner gliding down the smooth waters of the Ashley river to run the deadly gauntlet, at the proper moment. The bold seamen of these vessels had brought this dangerous business down to a science. The cunning captains on the darkest nights would run in and out of the tortuous channels of the harbor. A settled gloom rested on the city; the inhabitants moved about in the lower part like ghosts and the wierd shapes of tragedy. In some sections a citizen ran the risk of his life going abroad in daylight, so thievish and murderous had the rebel soldiers become. Stabbing, shooting and murder occurred daily. At our prison in Broad Street we had access to the papers, and had an opportunity to observe how matters were conducted in the lower section of Charleston, being allowed some liberty, under parole. Musket in hand these highwaymen (soldiers) patroled the streets seeking a victim;— streets now covered with long grass, once the busy scene of commerce and industry. The cobble-stones in what had once been the finest streets were completely concealed with rank weeds and grass. Goats and cows were to be seen quietly grazing on highways where, previous to the war, the rattling of wagons and the sound of passing vehicles could be heard day and night. The buzzard and the owl went to roost in concealed nooks once worn smooth with the passing tide of humanity. From gutters and low spots, once alive with progress and life, weeds and useless plants sprang four feet high, excluding from view the pavement on the other side of the street. The "cloud-capped towers and gorgeous palaces" had faded into a dream. Complete ruin, loneliness and desolation reigned in the city of secession, once the head and front of treason and rebellion. The remains of Capan and Palenque could scarcely recall sadder feelings of wreck, destruction and misery. I thought, as I looked on shattered houses, broken shafts and crumbling temples, of the few gallant boys enclosed in Sumpter in 1861 battling for the honor of their country against sixty thousand Southern braggarts, and exclaimed, "Unto thee, O God, do we give thanks, unto thee do we give thanks; for that thy name is near thy wondrous works declare."

About the 1st of October, 1864, the forces besieging Charleston mounted several new guns, two hundred pounders, that awakened the inhabitants to a sense of their insecurity. The missiles from these monsters could be heard whizzing and screaming, every few seconds, over the city. Every day people walking the streets were killed; halls and public buildings were knocked to pieces;

whole rows of houses were smashed into one complete mass of stone, brick and mortar. It was amusing to read the papers and hear the falsehoods told by the reporters! No damage was ever done! "only a goat or cow killed." One editor said, "It is remarkable that the enemy's shells never do damage; occasionally a goat or nigger is killed." When a fire broke out in the city, a strong guard was sent with each fire engine, who had orders to shoot those who were afraid to work. The papers would then state how gallantly the noble firemen extinguished the flames; they did not state "If they had not, death would have been their portion."

A good ride from Charleston was situated the Florence Prison pen, in which a large number of our men were confined, who had been brought from Andersonville. This jail was conducted in a style similar to that of Salisbury. No deed was too dark or bloody for its inhuman jailors. Men were starved and butchered as at Andersonville. One time there was not an ounce of food issued to the prisoners for three days, and in the next few days scores died of starvation; their last thoughts being of home and country; and their last words "*Bread! Bread!*" Men unable to stand on their feet, utterly prostrated for want of food, were brutally pushed into the ranks at roll-call by a bloodthirsty rascal called Sergeant Bush. There was a sneak and spy by the name of Fanbridge continually walking through camp, seeking a victim for his savage cruelty. There was also an unmerciful brute by the name of Barret who tortured many of our men. Day and night he was to be seen, walking through the prison, with a loaded revolver, cursing and threatening to shoot the helpless captives.

Many ingenious and daring attempts were made by officers to escape to our forces only a few miles distant. There were two successful escapes made from the city; these were accomplished by bribery, under guide of a Confederate soldier. It was a difficult matter, on account of the many rivers and inlets. Guards were stationed only a few yards apart for miles above Charleston down to Port Royal Ferry. Captains Lee and Nash, two intelligent and brave soldiers, after many trials, adventures and narrow escapes from drowning, were recaptured. They were out for days, and had gone only a few miles.

On the 6th of October, 1864, orders were given by General Hardee for our removal to Columbia, a small town in the interior, and capitol of the State. Hardee, after his many failures to stop the onward march of Sherman's brave boys, was placed in command of the prisons. Jeff. Davis no doubt thought if he could not fight armed men, he could surely kill the *unarmed*. Fifteen hundred prisoners, officers, were marched through the principal streets of the city to the depot, where they took the cars for Columbia. It was a wonderful sight; none will ever forget the parade of ragged and bearded men through King Street. One monster cursed us and a *lady* rebuked him, and said, "Don't taunt the poor fellows; God help them, it is a *pity* of them." The kind words went to all hearts and a "God bless *you*" came from every lip.

> "The quality of mercy is not strained;
> It droppeth, as gentle rain from heaven
> Upon the place beneath: it is twice bless'd;
> It blesseth him that gives, and him that takes:
> 'Tis mightiest in the mightiest; it becomes
> The throned monarch better than his crown."

CHAPTER XV.

Columbia Military Prison—Procuring Meat—Camp Sorghum—Food, Wood and Water—Rebel Atrocity—Lieutenant Parker Torn by Dogs—Escapes—Murder of Lieutenant Turbayne—Special Exchanges—Southern Robbers.

> "Never give up!—though the grape shot may rattle,
>   Or the full thunder-cloud over you burst,
> Stand like a rock,—and the storm or the battle
>   Little shall harm you, though doing their worst;
> Never give up!—if adversity presses,
>   Providence wisely has mingled the cup,
> And the best counsel, in all your distresses,
>   Is the stout watchword of Never give up."

The same kind of unventilated cattle-cars were employed in our transportation from Charleston to Columbia as had been formerly used in our various removals. A large number was piled in each car; and the individual was fortunate that obtained standing-room. All suffered for want of water, air and space. Nothing special occurred on the journey. Several of the prisoners eluded the vigilance of their guards and made their escape to the woods. Lieutenant Parker, who stood beside me in the car, intimated that as soon as it would be dark he would make an attempt to get away. About ten o'clock that night the Lieutenant made a spring past the guard, out of the car door, into the open air. The sentinel was very quick and fired his rifle, but missed the object. Giving vent to his feelings, he said:

"You'ens is mighty sharp; I was so kind to that ar' Yankee, I lit him sit on my blanket, and he played me such a cussed trick; you'ens can't do so no more!"

On a lot at Columbia, near the depot, we stopped a day and night, surrounded by a heavy guard. Most of the prisoners had no food, and being in a starving condition looked the picture of despair. About the time we left this place, a discovery was made of a large amount of bacon hanging to the rafters of a building that enclosed us on one corner. As the hungry men looked through the bars of a window and saw this meat, their eyes watered and their inventive faculties were aroused. Hooks, strings and poles were brought into requisition, and in a short time most of the meat, by Yankee talent, was transferred from the rafters of the building to the stomachs of the prisoners. Here an officer very nearly lost his life from a bayonet wound, inflicted by a brutal guard for overstepping an imaginary line. Whilst at the depot it rained heavily all night. The want of food and shelter in the rain-storm awakened the patriotism of the prisoners and kindled their ire against the rebels. Simultaneously every man burst out singing "Down with the Traitor." The rebels became alarmed, and reinforced the guard, and placed artillery in a prominent position to murder us, if it was deemed advantageous to their cause.

On the 8th of October we were moved about two miles from the town, and placed in an open field, containing four or five acres, with a few young pine trees to shade us. With a strong guard around us, we were turned loose to provide for ourselves. They issued neither axe, spade, nor cooking utensils. Two days after our arrival they pitched us some corn-meal and sorghum, the latter a substitute for molasses, which operated on the bowels like a dose of salts. For the first two weeks only a few were allowed to go in turns for wood, water, and to the sink. The sink was a terrible place of filth, and calculated to engender disease and cause death. A great many suffered from diarrhoea and dysentery, but were not permitted to visit the sink when occasion called and sank down in their uncleanness. Such inhuman and scientific brutality has no parallel in all the wars waged by savage nations. They have displayed some kindness to *sick* captives.

We had no quarters to protect us from the cold November storms, only huts made of brush and pine boughs. About the 1st of November they issued eight axes and as many shovels for fifteen hundred men. Many of the officers walked around all night to keep from freezing, and slept in the sun during the day. We went out under guard for wood once a day. As trees had to be cut down and axes were scarce, hundreds only obtained a few chips and broken branches. Several who had money gave one hundred dollars for an axe. A large number of officers burrowed in the ground. Several died for want of clothing and shelter. Our rations were miserable and not sufficient to sustain life. Two-thirds of the officers would have died of starvation had it not been for the money procured at Charleston by the power of attorney. We did not recive half the amount of food they pretended to issue for a certain number of days. They never issued one ounce of meat, nor a bucket or tub in which to wash. We never received a skillet or pot in which to cook. Our daily ration was:

    One pint of corn-meal, (cobb and all ground.)
    One-fifth of a pint of sorghum, (physic.)
    Three-quarters of a teaspoonful of salt.
    One square inch of soap.
    Occasionally a little flour or rice.

The treatment at this place was so brutal that every dark night starving heroes would run the guard and risk their lives to escape suffering and dying by inches with starvation. At this prison there was no stockade as at other rebel jails. The guards paced their beats on the ground, and on a level with those confined. Sometimes as many as forty would run the guard in one night. Generally some dashing soldier would act as leader, and rush past the sentinels, drawing their fire, in the imminent danger of losing his life, and his companions would join him before the guards would have their rifles reloaded. The rebels then would fire a volley into camp, killing or wounding some of the prisoners. Lieutenant Young of the Fifth Pennsylvania Cavalry was murdered by the ruffians whilst sitting at his hut. The poor man had been a prisoner twenty-two months; his hope was that he would live to see home. One night an officer lost his arm whilst running the guard. Lieutenant Ekings, of the Third Regiment New Jersey Volunteer Infantry, was shot through the heart whilst making arrangements with one of the guards for the escape of himself and companions. He was a generous, kind-hearted gentleman, and brave Christian soldier. When he was shot, the rebel scoundrels would not allow any of his friends near him to hear his dying words, or minister to his wants in his last moments. Through the influence of Captain Martin, rebel, a few of us were paroled and permitted to dig a grave and pay the last rites to the gallant Jersey Blue. He was my intimate friend. It was a solemn scene. A sadder duty I never performed to a deceased comrade. He had previously made his escape, but was recaptured in the mountains, after travelling one hundred and fifty miles, and returned to the prison where he met his death. About this time the rebels accidentally killed two of their own men, in their reckless shooting, and afterwards observed more care in firing at Yankees.

Hounds were kept near this prison, as at Andersonville and Macon, to track escaped fugitives.

One day two of the animals found their way into camp, but never left it alive. The rebels made many threats and were bitterly exasperated on seeing their favorite brutes dead. The owner said they were worth thousands of dollars, and cursed and swore like a fiend, calling down all the furies on the heads of the —— Yankees. As the animals were being taken out of camp, one of the prisoners shouted:

"As you have no fresh beef in this section of country, we thought it time to kill!"

This made them the more angry and our rations were cut down. Lieutenant Parker, mentioned in the beginning of this chapter, was so much torn and bitten by dogs that he died the day after his capture. Though there were many of the "chivalry" present with the dogs, not one called the brutes off, but on the contrary, encouraged their savage nature. On the 7th of November, 1864, a traitor captured an escaped prisoner, Lieutenant I. Clement. of the Fifteenth Kentucky Cavalry, and, after he had surrendered, hissed the blood-hounds on him. The poor man was so worried by the dogs that he was disabled for life. A Major Pascom was recaptured and savagely abused by the rascals. He asked to be treated as a prisoner of war, and was threatened with death. His hands were tied behind his back with a strong cord so tight that he fainted with extreme suffering. Many of the escaped officers recaptured were hung and murdered in the mountains. Outrages were perpetrated on the Union soldiers at which an Indian, in his savage state, would blush. Bodies were mutilated and cut into pieces. The remains of a captain from Ohio were found on the Blue Ridge disfigured in a shocking manner. His head and limbs were severed from his body and scattered about the place where he was murdered.

For several days, during the month of November, officers were paroled to go out of camp and procure wood. On two or three posts the guards were under the impression that nearly all were paroled. Hundreds, all who had shoes, or were able to walk, and *not* paroled, made the attempt to reach our lines. The country was full of escaped prisoners, and the wildest excitement prevailed among the inhabitants. Every county turned out its citizens to chase and hunt down the fugitives. Daily the tired and exhausted men were recaptured and returned to the prison; but many made their escape to our lines, after journeying hundreds of miles exposed to privation and suffering. Of all places in the South, where there was no regular military prison, Augusta, Georgia, was the worst. Prisoners after being caught were generally taken to this place and stripped of all their clothing, scarcely allowed to retain a rag to hide their nakedness. Hats, coats, shoes, and even shirts and pantaloons, were taken from the unfortunate captives who had no power of resisting the scoundrels. Two officers were knocked down and ironed, and given no food for two days because they refused to give up their shoes. Three men died from the effects of wounds received whilst resisting the guards in depriving them of their shirts. Officers and men were starved and murdered in a cotton warehouse near the river, for adhering to their flag and country.

On the morning of December first I was trying to kindle a fire with green wood to cook a pot of mush, when I was startled by the report of a rifle back of my hut. I jumped up and walked towards the imaginary dead-line and discovered that Lieutenant Turbayne, of the Sixty-sixth New York Volunteers, had been shot through the heart—murdered by a fiend called Williams, of Newbury Court-House, South Carolina. The soldier of the Union was shot whilst walking along a path that ran by the corner of a hut, but *inside of the dead-line*. Along this path the captives had walked since their entry into prison, without fear or molestation, as it was their own ground, a part of the field allotted to them for cooking, sleeping and walking, *not* outside of the prison bounds. Along this narrow way the Lieutenant was walking when the murderer brought his rifle to a ready and aim and ordered him back. The poor man turned and only walked a few steps, when the blood-thirsty scoundrel shot him through the back, the ball passing out of his bosom. He reeled, dropped to the earth, and died in a few minutes. Thus was an unarmed, faithful servant of the United States Government murdered by a villain styling himself a gentleman and South Carolinian. There was excitement and angry passion manifested by the officers in camp when the outrage became known. If the officer of the day had not relieved Williams, he would have been torn in pieces by the infuriated captives *no matter what the consequences would have been.* They said, "If we are to be shot down in this way, let us not die before we make our murderers feel the terrible vengeance of outraged nature." Now what did Major Griswold the commandant of the prison do with the murderer? He honored him! He not only refused to investigate the matter, but threatened the officer of the day with arrest for relieving Williams, and placed the murderer on duty, the afternoon of the same day, on the front line, and also sent him into camp next morning at roll-call, surrounded by a strong guard to prevent the officers from injuring his person. Major Griswold was a coward and possessed a contemptible spirit, or he never would have added insult to injury. It was said Williams was made a corporal for his heroism. It is a consolation to know if the rascal escapes the punishment due to his crime in this world, that in the next there is an Almighty Commander who will mete out justice.

Murder of Lieutenant Turboyne.

p. 150.

A ludicrous scene one day occured in camp. A very large hog happened to get through the guard-line, and when he was inside of the dead-line (in fact there was no dead-line; a small stake was driven in the ground here and there around camp, and none knew where the terrible line was) a rush was made for his porkship by the meat-hungry officers. In a shorter time than it would take to tell how, he was divided into hundreds of pieces.

> "The black hog was seen running through camp:
> Each man forgetting starvation and cramp,
> Grunts of the hog, and its running were vain—
> Never he'll be on that camp ground again."

About the first of December over one hundred sick and wounded left this camp for exchange; there were also fifty special exchanges. The policy of making special exchanges was condemned by nearly all; it seemed to be unjust, when all had risked their lives in the cause, to display partiality for some. Many were exchanged that had only been prisoners a few months, whilst sickly, starving men, who had been prisoners for nearly two years, were allowed to remain.

At roll-call the guards would steal any article the prisoners left in their huts. Several of the robbers were caught in the act, and when the rebel commandant was informed of it, he said, "Yankee prisoners have nothing; what they now possess belongs to my government."

A few shirts, drawers and towels were received

from the Sanitary Commission, also several packages of letters and three or four loads of boxes from friends in the North. Though many of the boxes were appropriated by the rebel officers, there was not as much rascality displayed in issuing them as at Libby Prison, Richmond.

Major I. H. Isett made many of the dreary hours pass pleasantly by singing patriotic and sentimental songs. He was a good singer. The following was a favorite piece of his:

>Don't stop a moment to think, John,
> Your country calls—then go;
>Don't think of me or the children, John,
> I'll care for them, you know.
>Leave the corn upon the stalks, John,
> Potatoes on the hill,
>And the pumpkins on the vines, John—
> I'll gather them with a will;
>But take your gun and go, John,
> Take your gun and go,
>For Ruth can drive the oxen, John,
> And I can use the hoe.
>
>I've heard my grandsire tell, John,
> (He fought at Bunker Hill,)
>How he counted all his life and wealth,
> His country's offering still.
>Shall we shame the brave old blood, John,
> That flowed on Monmouth Plain!
>No! take your gun and go, John,
> If you ne'er return again,
>Then take your gun and go, &c.
>
>Our army's short of blankets, John,
> Then take this heavy pair;
>I spun and wove them when a girl,
> And worked them with great care.

There's a rose in every corner, John,
    And there's my name, you see:
On the cold ground they'll warmer feel
    That they were made by me.
Then take your gun and go, &c.,

And if it be God's will, John,
    You ne'er come back again,
I'll do my best for the children, John,
    In sorrow, want, and pain.
In winter nights I'll teach them all
    That I have learned at school,
To love the country, keep the laws,
    Obey the Saviour's rule.
Then take your gun and go, &c.

CHAPTER XVI.

Insane Asylum Prison—An Ugly Face—Appearance of Prisoners—Food, Wood and Water—No Quarters—Suffering—Sickness—Drunken Doctors—Sutler's Prices—Bill of Exchange—Richland Jail—Incident of the Meal Sack—The Spy—Dr. Palmer, the Preaching Rebel—"Sherman's March to the Sea."

> "No fearing, no doubting, thy soldier shall know,
> When here stands his country, and yonder her foe;
> One look to the bright sun, one prayer to the sky,
> One glance where our banner floats glorious on high;
> Then on, as the young lion bounds on his prey;
> Let the sword flash on high, fling the scabbard away;
> Roll on, like the thunder-bolt over the plain!—
> We come back in glory, or come not again."

On the 12th of December, 1864, orders were received for our removal to the yard of the Insane Asylum, located in Columbia. We had been in so many prisons that this hasty order took none by surprise. Our route to the new prison lay through the city, and, as at other places, there was a large number of the citizens in the streets to view the procession. Many of the "snuff-dippers" were abroad, who gazed on us with neither compassion nor respect. One of the ugliest faces I have ever seen on the shoulders of the tender sex was protruded from the second story of a clothing establishment on the main street. Waving a handkerchief to our guards she screamed, with a voice resembling a night-hawk's:

"Sold'jars, don't let them 'uns run away."

One of the captives could not remain silent, and shouted:

"What a face! You should be North on exhibition; you would make a fortune in a short time."

There was a burst of laughter from all the prisoners, when a rebel officer cried in an angry tone:

"You'ens 'ill pay for insulting our *ladies*."

At the corner of one of the streets there was a man who had been drinking something stronger than water, and gave vent to his anger against Yankees in the most indecent and obscene language, and wanted to fight any prisoner in the crowd. A captain from Ohio told him to go to the front and he would get all the fighting he desired, when this disciple of Bacchus picked up a huge stone and threw it at the officer; but missing his object he struck a guard on the shoulder, who ran at him with his bayonet, and had he not made a hasty retreat, he would have received a just punishment for his cowardly attack.

Had the people of the North witnessed the ludicrous appearance of the captives, as they pursued their way through the principal streets of Columbia, they would not only have manifested sympathy, but would have smiled at the fantastic dresses and curious costumes which all wore; no two wearing a suit alike in shape or color. Some were in rags and had employed every means to hide their nakedness; others wore coats and pantaloons made from meal-bags and fifty different kinds of cloth, calico and muslin. Though the day was cold and disagreeable, many were shoeless and hatless, and some had their feet and heads tied up in worn out blue cloth, or old pieces of canvas. Every prisoner was loaded with something of no value to anybody but themselves, and would have been considered dirt in the house of a pauper. All struggled on with light hearts, carrying their pots, skillets, pieces of old stoves, (used as griddles,) bundles of rags, truck and trash, and believed that the time would soon come when the bogus Confederacy would fall to pieces.

On our arrival, and before our entrance into the yard, Major Griswold, the commandant, mounted a sentry box and made the following speech:

"Prisoners, you will now go within the enclosure;—you will be furnished with tools to build quarters. Around the yard is a board—the *deadline*—if you cross it, you will be shot, *and it will be taken out of your pay;*—if you destroy the tools, houses, trees or property, it will be taken out of your money in our hands.—Go in."

None could understand what he meant by saying "take it out of our pay." When we entered the yard it did not surprise us to find no trees, tools, little lumber, and only two dilapidated houses, and the frame of a barrack twenty-four feet square, divided into two rooms. The latter building was to be the model for the erection of quarters for the accommodation of the fifteen hundred officers. The wall, or stockade, of our prison was twelve feet high, built of brick on three sides, and a board fence separating us from the large building, or Asylum, containing *only a few* of the Insane men of the Southern States. Many of these men would shout and rave all night; and as some of the prisoners lay low with fever, and required quiet and rest, it was conduct in keeping with the previous brutality of the rebels to subject our poor fellows to this new species of outrage. There were three or four sentry boxes on each side of the prison-yard, elevated in a style similar to those at Macon. We were confined at this prison for over two months, and not one-third of the officers had quarters. Several old tents and pieces of canvas were brought in, which helped to cover the mouth of a hole burrowed into the ground by the helpless men and used as quarters, and in which it was impossible to remain in wet weather. Two thirds were without any kind of shelter whatever, *and in the dead of winter.* Hundreds were to be heard coughing during the whole night. It was bitter cold in January, and many nights the running water in the trough would be frozen eight and ten inches thick. As at Camp Sorghum, many walked around all night to keep from freezing, and slept in daytime. The ration of wood was of the meanest quality, and not as long nor as thick as a boy's arm for twenty-four hours; not near enough with which to cook our *mush*. Some days none would be issued, then there would be freezing and starving. There was great suffering at this pen during the long, cold, dreary and cheerless winter.

There was a plentiful supply of good water introduced to the prison-yard by means of a pipe and hydrant. All appreciated the luxury, and though impossible to wash clean, for lack of soap, the scrubbings and ablutions were taken often.

Our rations for five days at this prison were as follows:

- 3 Quarts of corn-meal, (cobb and all ground).
- 1 Gill of sorghum, (black, and disagreeable to the taste).
- 2 Table-spoonfuls of salt.
- 2 Table-spoonfuls of rice, (full of bugs and dirt).

We received two or three issues of black, dirty flour; one of corel and one of bran. At no time did we receive a ration of meat of any kind. We lived on meal and sorghum, consequently many of the officers had not sufficient strength to walk. The meal was made into a cake, or cooked into mush, and the sorghum poured over it. It was the roughest and poorest food men could eat to receive strength, and generally gave the diarrhoea and dysentery. For over two months I experienced much hardship and suffering from diarrhœa. In the dead of winter I would be up all hours of the night. I was poorly clad, and could get no food to give strength and tone to the stomach. There were five or six surgeons doing duty at this prison, but a more worthless or drunken crowd of men calling themselves *doctors* I have never seen. I could not receive the proper medicine for my disease. I received some kind of black pills that never did me the least good, and I ran the risk of my life every time I swallowed one. One morning I told the doctor I was no better, but worse, when he said:

"I cannot help it—I hav'nt got a drug store; you'll die in less than a week;—if one pill don't do you good, take half a dozen, and they will *kill or cure you.*"

I seldom visited him afterwards, and only when he was sober, which was not often. I did not expect to live to see my home. I had not the strength of a baby. When I would rise to my feet, my eyes would grow dim, and I would feel a dizziness in my head, and would be so weak I would stagger, and I was scarcely able to walk without help.

> "I miss thee, my mother, when young health has fled,
>   And I sink in the languor of pain.
> Where, where is the arm that once pillowed my head
>   And the ear that once heard me complain?"

My comrades, Adjutant Elkins, Captain Parker and Lieutenant Ramsey took the best possible care of me. For their humane and gentlemanly conduct, my heart will always be filled with gratitude, and my memory will ever cherish and keep green their names.

On the 4th of January, 1865, I had the good fortune to procure a bill of exchange, for one thousand dollars, made out on a responsible gentleman in the North, giving one dollar in gold for ten dollars in Confederate money. I received an order on the sutler for the amount. Afterwards I had a change of diet, and gradually picked up, regaining my health and strength, and possessed a supply of the rebel trash while in the Confederacy. There was an opportunity to procure potatoes, wheat bread, meat, vinegar and salt, and other necessary articles. I had up to this time been without shoes, and bought a pair of English brogans, for which I gave over one hundred dollars. I also bought a shirt for thirty dollars that would not cost as many cents in the North; also a tooth-brush for twelve dollars worth about six cents. Extravagant prices were asked for everything. Dollars in the Confederacy were not valued as high as cents in the North. Enormous prices had to be paid for even the commonest articles. The following is a list of sutler's prices at Columbia, South Carolina.

Sweet potatoes, $35.00 per bushel.
Bread, 6 oz. loaves, $1.50.

Beef, $5.00 per lb.   Pork, $7.00 per lb.
Eggs, $12.00 per dozen.
Lard, $16.00 per lb.
Butter $20.00 per lb.
Salt, $3.00 per lb.
Segars, $1,00 each.
Foolscap paper, $225,00 per ream.
Sole leather, $45,00 per lb.
Tea, $120,00 per lb.
Sheeting, $10,00 per yard.
Nutmegs, $2,50 each.
Thread, $1,50 per small skein.
Combs, common, $15,00 (very scarce.)
Shoes, English army, $125,00 per pair.
Smoking tobacco, $10,00 per lb.
Playing cards, $36,00 per pack.
Tooth brushes, $12,00 each.
White blankets, $400,00 per pair.
Lead pencils, $3,00 each.
Candles $22,00 per lb.
Socks, scarce, $14,00 per pair.
Black pepper, $35,00 per lb.
Brown sugar, $18,00 per lb.
No coffee in market.

All these articles were of the poorest quality. Sutlering was on the same style at all the prisons, with some variation in prices. Base men resorted to cunning and roguish plans to extort money from the captives. There was but *one* place to purchase articles. The sutler obtained his price, no matter what he asked. The prisoner who would not buy from him could obtain it nowhere else. The sutler, grinning, would say:

"The money is worthless: when I go to market I take a horse and wagon to carry the money, and what I buy I am able to carry home in a basket."

He was about half right, for the country was flooded with the trash; it must have kept every printing press in the Confederacy busy striking off the truck. Before I left the Confederacy one dollar in gold would bring one hundred and twenty-five dollars of Southern money, and a one dollar greenback over eighty dollars of Confederate money. Several of the wealthy men of South Carolina saw the Confederacy was going to pieces, and to save themselves from utter ruin, came into the prison and bought Bills of Exchange on Northern houses. These Southern braggarts could revile Northern people and their government, but still desired Uncle Sam's gold and greenbacks. During the latter part of my stay at this prison nearly all the officers seemed to have plenty of money. At all hours of the day a motley crowd of prisoners was to be seen in different parts of the enclosure engaged in "Bucking the tiger." As at Macon, gambling was carried on in this prison extensively; hundreds of dollars changed hands in a few seconds.

About the centre of the town of Columbia was situated the Richland Jail, in which one hundred and twenty-five Federal officers had been confined during the summer and fall, when they were transferred to the Asylum Prison with us, on our removal from Camp Sorghum. They had been treated very badly, and suffered in body and mind; many of them had not sufficient clothing to hide their nakedness. A brave captain from Tennessee, for his ardent patriotism and strong love of country, was kept in irons at this prison for *nineteen months*.

Some of the captives had appropriated mealsacks to make pantaloons and shirts, and construct some kind of shelter from the weather. Every few days a sergeant with a guard came into the prison tearing down miserable quarters, and carrying off every old rag that had marked on it "Tax in kind;" articles useless to every one only prisoners situated as we were. One day the sergeant, going through the yard seeking sacks, spied a shirt that had just come out of the wash, and on it the words "Tax in kind." The sergeant was about to seize the article, but the owner who had been observing him, caught hold of it before him, and hastily tore a piece off the garment and presented it to him, saying:

"The shirt is made of sheeting I bought at the sutler's; but as I did not have sufficient material to finish it, I thought *your* government liberal and rich enough to supply a *tail!*"

A roar of laughter greeted the remark, and the sergeant did not seek any more rags that day on which were the words "Tax in kind."

To prevent the meal-sacks from being appropriated or lost, some workmen came into the prison and constructed us a "feed-box," into which our rations were emptied, as though every man in the yard was a *hog*. The plan did not last long: in less than one week the "feed-box" was broken up and used for kindling wood.

At this prison several tunnels in course of construction were discovered. A man called Saber was suspected of giving information to the rebels: it was said he was an enlisted man, and had passed into the prison as an officer on false representation. Had he not been taken out of the prison at the time of the discovery he would have been hung. If he was not a traitor to his companions, he was at least a disgrace; for every rebel official that came into the yard, he would follow around, currrying favors and doing actions of which no gentleman or officer would be guilty. The following notice was posted in a conspicuous place in the prison:

> Prisoners of War will take notice that I am directed by General Winder, commanding prisoners of war, to say that in case any more tunneling takes place in this prison, he will remove all the barracks and tents, so that it will be the fault of the prisoners themselves if they have no covering from the weather.

They will further take notice, if any injury is done

to any fellow prisoner, suspected of giving information, I shall use force for force,—and the guilty party will be punished.

     E. GRISWOLD,
        Major Com'ding Prison.

Two-thirds of the officers had neither "barracks nor tents," and the latter paragraph reads as if a tell-tale had been in our midst.

A passionate Frenchman had command of the prisoners for a few days. The first day he took charge, he had us drawn up in line and gave utterance to the following words in broken English:

"I takes command now.—I's expects behaviour from officers and men. I's been a prisoner to Fort Delaware nine months. You's made us behave. I's make you behave. Break ranks.—March."

A few days after he assumed the responsibility of the prison, he had a quarrel with a rebel surgeon and called him a liar; he was relieved of his command. This man had given orders to the guards to shoot the negro, who occasionally came into the prison, if he was seen talking to the prisoners.

Confined in this prison was a veritable Count by the name of Braiday. He had neither hat nor shoes, and was clad in rags. The notorious rebel Dr. Palmer, the first to advocate secession in New Orleans, preached for us twice. He had for his texts, "Only Believe;" "The Great Promise." Most of the officers passed the dreary hours in innocent amusements. Lieutenant Chandler and three other officers succeeded in obtaining a bass violin and three other instruments, and in good weather they gave concerts, which brought to our prison animation, life and mirth, and hastened many of the sad, sorrowful days of our confinement. Some evenings there would be singing and dancing, accompanied with music; on these occasions rebel officers would place their lady friends in the sentry boxes to "show off the live Yankees." No Northern lady could be induced to visit such a "pen" under the circumstances; but Southern women only blush at their own immodesty.

The following beautiful and expressive song was written by Lieutenant Byers, Adjutant of the Fifth Iowa Cavalry, while a prisoner at Columbia, and sung by Major Isett and three officers with good taste and thrilling effect:

> Our camp fires shone bright on the mountains
>   That frowned on the river below;
> While we stood by our guns in the morning,
>   And eagerly watched for the foe;
> When a rider came out of the darkness,
>   That hung over mountain and tree,
> And shouted: "Boys up, and be ready,
>   For Sherman will march to the sea!"
>
> Then cheer upon cheer for bold Sherman,
>   Went up from each valley and glen,
> And the bugle re-echoed the music,
>   That came from the lips of the men;
> For we knew that the stars in our banner,
>   More bright in their splendor would be,
> And that blessings from Northland would greet us,
>   When Sherman would march to the sea.

Then "Forward, boys; forward to battle!"
  We marched on our wearisome way;
And we stormed the wild hills of *Resacca!*
  God bless all who fell on that day;
Then Kennesaw, dark in its glory,
  Frowned down on the Flag of the Free;
But the East and the West bore our standard,
  As Sherman marched down to the sea.

Still onward we pressed, till our standard
  Swept out from Atlanta's grim walls;
And the blood of the Patriot dampened
  The soil where the traitor flag falls:
But we paused not to weep for the fallen,
  Who slept by each river and tree,
Yet we twined them a wreath of the laurel
  As Sherman marched down to the sea.

Proud, proud was our army that morning,
  That stood by the cypress and pine,
When Sherman said, " Boys, you are weary,
  This day fair Savannah is thine !"
Then sang we a song for our chieftain,
  That echoed o'er river and lea,
And the stars on our banner shone brighter,
  When Sherman marched down to the sea.

CHAPTER XVII.

"Sherman's Coming"—Excited Rebels—Southern Despotism—The Braggart South Carolinians—The Cadets—A Prison Brings Grey Hairs—The Dead Winder and the Living Wirz—Escapes and Hardships—The Union League—The Poor Union Woman.

> "'Mid the din of arms, when the dust and smoke
>   In clouds are curling o'er thee,
> Be firm till the enemy's ranks are broke,
>   And they fall, or flee before thee!
> But I would not have thee towering stand
>   O'er him who's for mercy crying,
> But bow to the earth, and with tender hand
>   Raise up the faint and dying."

On the morning of the 13th of February, 1865, our Asylum Prison, Columbia, was thrown into a boisterous state of excitement and joy by the thunder of the cannon of Sherman's advance guard. Bustle, animation and mirth seized our jail, and the hope of a release took possession of the hearts of the captives. Sickly men became well; drooping spirits revived; those heretofore unable to walk nervously paced their contracted bounds with flashing eyes and smiling countenances. The question was "Where will they take us to now?" In the South and West all their rail-road connections were severed; so if we were removed, and not released, we would have to be transported into North Carolina or Virginia, and there the combined armies of Sherman and Grant would soon scatter and demolish the remaining demoralized armies of the traitors. Daily the Confederacy was growing smaller and weaker. The material for their armies was completely gone. The ruthless conscription act of the conspirators had seized old and young; "robbed the cradle and the grave." Gray haired men, scarcely able to walk, and bent with age, were violently dragged from their homes and muskets placed in their hands to serve a bad cause. Boys and children that required watching and care were torn from the paternal roof and placed in the ranks of the traitors to fight against the flag under which they were born. The bloody iron heal of a military despotism reigned over every county and State not held by our troops, grinding into dust the weak and strong if they offered resistance to the edicts of the dark-minded rebels; breaking up the tender ties of parental affection, and crushing the most endeared feelings of the human heart. As the Confederacy became weaker and smaller, tyranny and wrong, outrage and murder grew more desperate, bold and bloody, and no act was too dark, or crime too horrid for the rebel government to commit. The bounds of the Confederacy were fast narrowing and our long-range guns would soon be able to send their deadly missiles completely through the bogus concern—over all the territory they possessed. They would soon be like one of the small states of Germany that determined to put its army upon a war footing, and resolved to purchase the most improved weapons of war, and accordingly procured an Armstrong gun upon trial. Having got the gun a great difficulty arose—they had no place to put up the target. Their own space of territory was not large enough; and as none of the neighboring States were willing to allow it to be put up in theirs, the trial had to be foregone. This was becoming the case with the rebels. They could erect no target in any State which they claimed, that the soldiers of the Union could not demolish. This was a cause of rejoicing for every lover of his country but more *especially* to the hungry, naked and dying captives, who had been confined for years, and felt the effects of *Southern* treatment. Prisoners felt satisfied and content when they could hear the rebels were being beaten and scattered on every hand. They, the rebels, would lie, and tell us their army was gaining great battles, going where they pleased and conquering all opposed to them, and did all that lay in their power to keep the news of their own defeats from reaching us, but we could always, by some means, get the true version of affairs. When the thunder of Sherman's cannon was heard in Columbia, the rebels said it was one of their batteries practising; but the captives felt an inward joy and told the traitors it was some of Sherman's *practising*, putting the fear of the Lord into their rebel hearts. When the order came to remove us to North Carolina, the rebels said it was for exchange, in order to prevent officers from attempting to escape, and to conceal the fact that Sherman's troops were only a short distance from the city. The prisoners did not believe this exchange rumor, but felt hopeful and said:

> "Tramp, tramp, tramp, the boys are marching;
> Cheer up, comrades, they will come,
> And beneath the starry flag we shall breathe the air again
> Of the free land in our own beloved home."

On the night of February 13th, a rainy, dreary and cheerless night, we were taken from the Asylum Prison to the rail-road depot, about six squares from the pen. After waiting one hour at the depot, standing in the street ankle-deep in mud during a violent storm, it was found out that the cowardly citizens of Columbia had taken possession of the train and departed, when they heard of the approach of Sherman's legions. At all times the boastful citizens of South Carolina were the first to run in times of danger, as they were the braggart leaders in talk against the Federal Government at the beginning of the war. In Sherman's grand march through the Southern States he found less opposition in South Carolina than in any other State. The poltroons and Falstaffs of the Palmetto State could talk and run, but not fight. The only action in which the South Carolinians distinguished themselves during the war, without running, was when sixty thousand of them took Fort Sumpter held against them by one hundred men. The rebel commandant, after indulging in much boisterous talk, cursing and swearing, took us back to our unclean quarters in the Asylum yard. A company of cadets formed a part of the guard that accompanied us to the depot and back to the prison. In their education they had been spoiled; and though they prided themselves on their gentlemanly appearance, a more contemptible band of young men never carried arms. Continually swearing, they were abusive and insulting. There was not a spark of humanity or mercy in their composition. Crossing a gutter I fell into the mud, when one of the rascals made a thrust at me with his bayonet; he missed my leg, but made a hole in my pantaloons He made his lunge out with such force that if I had been struck I would in all probability have lost my limb or life. One prisoner was struck on the head with the rifle of another of the dastardly knaves, and will carry to his grave a huge scar.

It is astonishing to witness the effect confinement has on the hair and beard of some of the captives. If civilians were imprisoned and subjected to the treatment our soldiers received while prisoners, eighteen out of every twenty would die. Nearly all those who had been in the service only a few weeks and were imprisoned in Southern pens died It was hard to kill our gallant soldiers who had been inured to hardship and adventure, heat and cold, hunger and thirst. Soldiers in the field, in time of war, become intimate with these, but *prisoners* grow familiar with every species of misery and wretchedness. A number of the captives whose heads and beards were glossy and black when they entered a Southern prison, had grown quite gray since their confinement. One officer's hair turned completely gray in a few weeks. He spent much of his time walking up and down the contracted limits of his prison. He was a *young* man, but care, misery and bad treatment in prison, had altered his looks—changed his appearance and figure. Young in years he was old looking in his shape, features, and movements. The prison, and not time, had brought gray hairs to hundreds of dark heads, and wrinkled the faces of scores of handsome men.

> "Danger, long travel, want or woe,
> Soon change the form that best we know;
> For deadly fear can time outgo,
> And blanch at once the hair;
> Hard time can roughen form and face,
> And what can quench the eye's bright grace,
> Nor does old age a wrinkle trace,
> More deeply than despair."

Whilst at the Asylum Prison the announcement was made that General J. H. Winder was dead. Is it wrong to feel elated over the death of a fellow man and foe? Every heart in the prison beamed with joy, and every heart rejoiced in the thought that this demon was no more. We had all suffered from his diabolical plans to systematically starve us, and felt that a good God had taken the breath from this vile man as punishment for his awful crimes. If two murderers ever desecrated the fair earth they trod, they were the dead Winder and the living Wirz. May a wise Providence put it into the hearts and minds of those trying the inhuman brute and coward in Washington to mete out justice to him, and visit upon his head some swift punishment which he so richly deserves. The companions of the martyred dead who bared their bosoms on the high places of the field for the country's salvation, and stood shoulder to shoulder in many a bloody fray demand it. The relatives of the noble starved respectfully ask it, and *will have it!*

> "Who dies in vain
> Upon his country's war-fields and within
> The shadow of her altars? Feeble heart!
> I tell thee that the voice of patriot blood,
> Thus pour'd for faith and freedom hath a tone
> Which from the night of ages, from the gulf
> Of death shall burst and make its high appeal
> Sound unto earth and heaven!

The companion of one of my friends was returned to the Asylum Prison, when recaptured in the mountains, after travelling hundreds of miles and enduring incredible privations and hardships Clothed as a rebel soldier, he and two associates journeyed through the country, procuring food at planters' houses. When in company of rebels he tyrannized over his companions, who were attired in what had once been Federal uniforms, and passed them off as his prisoners. When asked where he was taking his captives, he said to Greenville for close confinement. Passing through several counties of western South Carolina they gained the Tennessee mountains, where they were discovered by a band of guerillas and pursued. For safety, and as a last resort to gain their freedom, they parted company, each one taking his own road. One reached the Federal lines more dead than alive; the second was never heard of, probably was retaken and murdered, or perhaps died of exposure, fatigue and starvation; the third was placed in the Asylum Prison yard.

In many of the large towns in the Southern States there were societies organized for the purpose of assisting the Union cause when opportunities offered. Savannah, Charleston, and Columbia, and other cities and towns had their Union League meeting rooms. Under the severe and relentless military despotism of the Southern traitors these faithful men could never accomplish any grand enterprise, such as throwing off the yoke of their tyrants, and raising the old flag they loved and respected; they, however, did much good in keeping alive a spirit of hostility against rebels, giving them trouble, and causing the Confederate Government to keep a military force in the interior, which otherwise could have been of service at the front. Many of our soldiers who escaped from the various prisons in the South were taken care of by the League. They secreted two of our officers in Charleston for four weeks, and finally secured the services of a guide who took them in safety into the Union lines. Many of our officers who made their escape by way of the Tennessee mountains were clothed, fed and piloted across the country and through their dangerous route by these staunch lovers of the Union.

On the 14th of February, 1865, we were closed in the cattle-cars, the smallest and most unclean we had yet occupied, and took our departure for Charlotte, North Carolina, amidst the greatest excitement that ever took place in the capital of South Carolina. Men and women, young and old, were hurrying from the town in buggies, wagons, and all descriptions of vehicles, out of Sherman's path. They said the ubiquitous General would burn the town, commit violence, hang and cut into pieces the old women and children. "Yes," said one of the prisoners to the excited rebels, "Sherman *is* coming, and he will give you a few lessons before he leaves you; but why don't you stop him?" The remark irritated the already angry feelings of the rebels. Before leaving the depot, a poor woman slipped into my hand a piece of bread, saying,

"I'm glad they're coming; I cannot do more for you,—God bless you."

Tears came into my eyes, and I had scarcely time to thank the poor, brave Union woman, when a brutal guard seized her dress and dragged her to the other side of the street. None live but can at least try to do some good.

> If you can not in the conflict
>   Prove yourself a soldier true;
> If, where fire and smoke are thickest,
>   There's no work for you to do;
> When the battle-field is silent,
>   You can go with careful tread,
> You can bear away the wounded,
>   You can cover up the dead.

M

CHAPTER XVIII.

Southern Railroads—Accidents—Fresh Beef—Exchange Rumors—"Snuff Dippers"—Murder of Captain Evens—Prison at Charlotte—Story of an Escape—Oath of Allegiance Men—Paroled—Homeward—What a Secessionist thought of a Copperhead—Break Down—Raleigh—Goldsborough—Suffering Union Boys—In our own Lines.—Joy.

> How sleep the brave, who sink to rest,
> By all their country's wishes blest;
> When spring, with dewy fingers cold,
> Returns to deck their hallow'd mould,
> She there shall dress a sweeter sod,
> Than fancy's feet have ever trod.
> By fairy hands their knell is rung,
> By forms unseen their dirge is sung,
> There honor comes, a pilgrim gray,
> To bless the turf that wraps their clay,
> And freedom shall awhile repair,
> To dwell a weeping hermit there.

Towards the close of the rebellion it was very dangerous travelling on Southern railroads. The rolling stock on nearly all the roads was worn out and the greatest care had to be observed in running trains in order to prevent a smash, or accident; the boilers of the engines, once the best quality, were nearly gone, and it was only by good management the engineers were able to keep the rickety concern together, or by ingenious skill ward off break-downs. All the tracks were shaky and completely worn.

Whilst a prisoner I travelled about two thousand miles on the Southern roads, and never three hundred miles but there was a break-down of some description. On one of these roads a number of Federal prisoners, enlisted men, were killed and wounded, through the carelessness of those having the train in charge, or a reckless and mulish disposition of the officials of the Rebel Government to carry on the transportation of their bogus concern. The sweeping conscription act had taken the working men and mechanics, and left the founderies and machine shops with few or no hands whatever, and they were generally men detailed from the army. The roads were burthened to their fullest capacity with the transportation of supplies and the transfer of troops from one department to another; consequently, the roads and rolling-stock wore out, and there being neither material nor laborers with which to make repairs, the Southern rail-roads in reality became killing machines. When about half a day's ride from Columbia, our train ran into a drove of cattle lying on the track, that were being driven out of Sherman's path. Three cows were killed, and the engine thrown off the track, and some important part of its machinery broken. An Almighty Father prevented a frightful accident. Hundreds of lives might have been lost, and scores terribly mangled, in a country where there would have been neither sympathy, pity nor love displayed by the inhabitants. It was an act of Providence, for the animals were butchered and divided among the prisoners; this was the first meat, of any description, the Rebel Government had issued to us for *one hundred and thirty three days.* For *four months* from these inhuman men we only received meal and sorghum. Southern men will lie, and their sympathisers, the Copperheads of the North, will try to throw a screen over their dark doings, but Time, that great revealer of all things, brings to light and shows to the world the unmerciful actions of these bad men. The accident was a Providential occurrence, for in place of bringing death it brought food and life.

Where this accident occurred was the first place we received notice of the order for our exchange. Major Griswold went to the door of every box-car and read a telegraph despatch from the rebel Secretary of War, ordering our removal into North Carolina for exchange. Though the Federal officers had no respect for this bad man, who failed to punish the murderer of one of their companions, they listened attentively whilst he read the stirring despatch, and did not give it credit, but believed it to be a ruse of his own invention to prevent officers from making an attempt to escape.

During the remainder of the time taken to reach Charlotte nothing special occurred on the route. At one of the stations I saw several ladies, "snuff-dippers," shake their closed hands at us; others assumed an air of modesty, but their faces reminded me of school-days when mischievous boys made ugly faces at the teacher's back. The men had nothing to say; they would turn pale when the prisoners said, "Sherman's coming!"

At Charlotte we remained in the cars all night. We were packed in so close, we suffered for want of air and room, and had to stand up all night. An officer, Captain Evans, lost his life in attempting to escape by the bottom of the car. He was shot in the leg and died from the effects of amputation. The inhuman guard in place of telling the man to go back, or pricking him with the point of his bayonet, put the muzzle of his rifle close to the poor fellow's limb when he fired.

> "Butchers and villains, bloody cannibals!
> How sweet a plant have you untimely cropp'd!
> You have no children, butchers! if you had,
> The thought of them would have stirr'd up remorse."

About half a mile from the rail-road we were placed in a field, with a guard around us. Our prison consisted of a piece of woods, a few old, torn tents, and a rickety shanty that had once been a barn.

The prison was called Camp Bacon, from the fact of its being the first place where a meat ration was issued for nearly five months. The ground selected for our prison was badly located and unhealthy, and calculated to cause chills and fever; the weather was disagreeable and stormy, yet the captives zealously went to work burrowing, making houses of pine boughs, and getting quarters as comfortable as possible. While here, we were under command of Captain Stewart, of Frederick City, Maryland, who treated us as "prisoners of war," and did what he could to alleviate our suffering condition,—what no other rebel ever did who had charge of us. At this prison there was a strip of woods in which the rebels neglected to place a guard, and for a few hours after our arrival hundreds of the captives, all who knew of it and were well, and possessed shoes, made their escape through this opening. Nearly all of the poor fellows were afterwards recaptured.

The following letter I received from an old prison friend, in which he gives a graphic description of his escape with several others from the prison pen at Charlotte:

PHILADELPHIA, *Oct. 3d,* 1865.

FRIEND FERGUSON:—I promised to give you the details of my escape from the rebels. I lost my journal and consequently will have to write from memory. But I would have a poor memory indeed did I not remember some of the incidents which occurred while I was within the rebel lines, especially while attempting to escape at different times, for you know my last was the sixth effort I made for liberty. You know how the booming of Sherman's artillery sent the blood coursing through the veins of us wretched prisoners; how many an eye grew bright that for a year before had been dull; how we all got "Escape on the Brain." Well, I was one among the number who made up my mind to escape.

There was no opportunity to get away from the rebels between Columbia and Charlotte.

After going into camp at Charlotte the chance occurred. I took a look at the camp to see which would be the best way to get out. You remember at one end of the camp (and inside of the line of sentinels) there was a little wood, or thicket, and I thought this was the best place to make my exit. I went into it, and by dint of dodging and hiding, and waiting and crawling, I got outside the line of sentinels. Once outside the line, I took to running towards a wood at some distance. I looked back once to the camp I had left to see if I was pursued, when, to my utter astonishment, instead of the rebels I expected to see, the field which I had just passed over was covered with blue jackets. They were on the same business as myself, trying to escape. There must have been three hundred got out that day, and you know how difficult it is to escape even after eluding the guards; for not as many as fifty of that number made good their escape—the rest were recaptured, some killed, their friends will never know how nor where. At a distance of about a mile from the prison camp nearly all who got out assembled in groups of from three to twenty; none spoke above their breath. Then commenced a picking of companions for the journey. Nearly all I spoke to were in favor of making in the direction of Sherman's lines. I thought if so many went in that direction that it would be a poor chance for any to get through. I was in favor of going in the direction of Tennessee. By a great deal of argument and persuasion I at last got Captain Robinson, of the sixty-seventh Pennsylvania Infantry, Lieutenant Frank Hubble of the same and Captains Derbrow and Gilbert of New York Regiments to consent to go in the direction of Tennessee; hoping to find Colonel Kirk's command in the neighborhood of Morganton, North Carolina; (having been informed by a negro that he was there.) We started, but found it rather difficult, as none of us knew the exact direction of Morganton. By good fortune we stumbled on Lieutenant Henry of the Fifth Ohio Cavalry, who happened to have a piece of the map of North Carolina with Morganton and Charlotte on it, from which we took a copy. We started in pursuit of the Morganton road. Having found the road, the next important matter was if possible to get something to eat. The three previous days I had but two crackers, and they were given me by a rebel private (*he was one more generous than the rest*) My companions were as badly in want of food as myself. Lieutenant Hubble and myself were selected by the party to hunt food, as we had the most experience in that line, on account of our frequent attempts to escape. We accordingly went "scouting," as we called it, in the same old fashioned way that all prisoners trying to escape in the South have done; first, find a house, (which at times is difficult) next find the little cabin, which is not hard to do, once having found the big house. It is useless to say the big house is the residence of the master, the cabin the residence of the slave. The slave is the man, or woman, we are looking for; the master is the man we are to avoid. The slave will give us something to eat, and get out of his cabin at midnight to guide us to liberty; the master will get out of his bed at midnight to chase us with his bloodhounds. The master is of our own race; the slave is not. The black man is our friend; the white man is our enemy. We approached a cabin cautiously for fear of waking the dogs at the big house, as life and liberty depended on every step. We reached the cabin, and looked in through the logs, and could see forms, but so indistinctly we did not know whether they were white or black people. Some one spoke inside; we could not go in there as there were white men in the cabin. We waited awhile for them to go away. Perhaps they were not white men. We looked again, and found they were rebel soldiers with guns and accoutrements. The above will give a pretty good idea of how an escaping prisoner has to manage to get anything to eat. Our attempt the first night to get something to eat was a failure. So we walked on towards Morganton in rather down-cast spirits till nearly morning, when seeing at some distance from the road a barn, we decided to go in and lay down and sleep. I assure you we were all soon asleep

It did not seem to me a minute from the time I lay down till I was waked up by something pulling my feet. I waked to hear and see a negro girl screaming. I very soon quieted her, however, by telling her that we were Yankees, and told her to send a colored man to us if there was one about the plantation. She went back to the house and sent a colored man with some corn bread and meat, which we soon devoured. He showed us a place in a swamp where we could stay all day hid from view.

We did as he told us, and selected a dry spot. We got some wood, struck a fire with flint and a knife, dried our clothes, which were very wet, and felt more comfortable than we did the previous day. At dark that evening (according to agreement with the colored man,) we went back to the barn, where he had a plentiful supply of victuals for us.

Our appetites satisfied better than for at least six months before, we started for a ferry on the Catawba River, called "Connor's Mills," which we reached about daylight on the next morning.

We had recourse again to our old way of getting something to eat, by going to the darkies' cabins. We were more successful in this effort than in our first attempt. Again a darky piloted us to a place of safety for the day time and brought us plenty to eat. In fact there was not a negro, male or female, within seven miles, that did not visit us that day, each one contributing something for our comfort, because we were Yankees; and that night they took us across the Catawba River in a canoe, and gave us all the information they could regarding the roads, and one of them went with us about eight miles to flank some rebel picket posts, when if we had gone without a guide, we would in all probability have been recaptured.

Our troubles at this time commenced; it rained five days in succession. We walked at night time altogether, and in the day time we would go into the woods, make a fire and lay there until it got dark, when we would again start on our journey, hungry, cold, wet, and tired. I cannot forbear relating an incident that occurred at one of the fordings of the Catawba.

It was a very cold night, and we had walked about twenty-five miles to reach the ford before daylight; having reached it, the question was how we were to get to the other side, as the river was very much swollen by the recent rains; after some talk about making a raft, it was decided that as I was the tallest of the party I should attempt to ford it; which I accomplished, the water reaching over my shoulders; the others immediately followed me. When we arrived on the opposite side we did not have a dry stitch on our backs. It was freezing very hard and our tinder that we usually made our fires with was wet, so we were in the most wretched condition. In this miserable plight we walked about five or six miles; our clothes were as stiff as pasteboard with frost. Having been made desperate with suffering, we decided to ask admission at the first house we met.

Hearing a rooster crowing, we followed in the direction of the sound, hoping thereby to find a habitation, which we succeeded in doing. Just as we reached the house, the man was making the customary log fire, by which we dried our clothes and warmed ourselves. The man was one of those busy, meddling old fellows, and asked us who we were, where we were going, and what we intended doing. We answered that we were scouts, and were going up to the mountains after the "Tories." This pleased the old chap very much, and he told us not to spare one of them, to kill all.

He cursed the Yankees generally, but dwelt with particular bitterness on General Burnside and Colonel Kirk, (the latter a Union man of North Carolina.) We assisted the old fellow to abuse the Yankees, and we did it so well that before we left his house he suspected that we were not all right.

When we left the house, we were pretty sure of being chased by dogs and all the Cavalry Home Guards; so, instead of going ahead on our course, we went about three hundred yards from his house into the woods, built a fire, and stayed there all day. It was well for us that we took this course; for in half an hour after, they were in full pursuit of us, but they went in the wrong direction.

In something like this manner we pursued our course from day to day until we got near the mountains; then we met white men that were glad to see us and assist us. The Union men of west North Carolina and East Tennessee can never be paid for their devotion to the Government of the United States. It was very easy to be a Union man and a lover of country in the North, but in the Southern States it was death; consequently, nearly all the Union men were "Bushwhackers," or "Layers-out," as they were called. I will never forget my first introduction to one of these men. But I will tell you. It was our first day in the mountains, and the Union people told us to be very careful; that is, the women told us, none of the men being at home, for the rebel cavalry from Lenoir were up conscripting, and they expected bad work. Hearing of the cavalry being so near, made us more cautious, so we took the small paths over the mountains. We were going through a place called the Rich Lands, a great Union district, and worse for our purpose at that time, as the cavalry spoken of would be sure to visit it to conscript. The path on which we were walking made a sudden turn to the left, and just before us stood a man in a blue hunting shirt, with a long rifle pointed at us, demanding, in a very cool way, who we were. We answered, after taking a long breath, the simple word "Yankees." He took his gun from his shoulder, sat himself on a rock, and exclaimed, *So am I!* We shook hands with him, when he told us it was well for us that we answered as we did, or we would all have been killed. I will here state that nearly all of our party were dressed in rebel clothes. Hamlet was the name of the individual.

He told us that the mountains were full of such men as himself, and he was an out and out rebel hater and bushwhacker.

I thought his name was fictitious; but when he took us to his father's house I discovered it was his real name, and though he had never heard of the "melancholy Prince of Denmark," he knew "a hawk from a heron."

That night we held a sort of jubilee at the house of his father. Hamlet, though having a princely name, was anything but princely in wealth; so we went to the house of an old gentleman named Harrison, a good Union man, who supplied us with provisions.

After this we met many of the bushwhackers. A more manly and daring set of men I have never met; they all treated us with kindness. The next day we again set forth in better condition and spirits than we had any day since we commenced the journey. Hamlet was our guide.

We expected at this time to meet our forces in "Crab-Orchard," Tennessee, a distance of about one hundred miles from the "Rich Lands," N. C. It was rather difficult to leave where we were, as the rebel cavalry were picketing the roads; by going a good distance out of the direct way, however, we avoided them. Hamlet knew all the Union people along our route, which was a great advantage to us, for they supplied us with the information we needed, and also with provisions. We were delayed for three days on account of a horrid murder that was perpetrated by Miller's Cavalry from Lenoir Not satisfied with shooting an old man, but whilst he had life, they dragged him with a rope for five miles, then put him in the woods where they left him to linger and die of their brutality. When he was found, three days after, his entrails were torn away, and his breast eaten by the wolves. In fact, there was scarcely enough of him left to be recognized by his wife, who was the person that discovered him. The man's name, who was thus brutally murdered for being "a Union man," was Coffee. This murder roused the Union men and bushwhackers, and they determined to fight the cavalry that perpetrated it, and for that purpose we remained three days in a "Rock-House," (an institution well known to the Union people of North Carolina and Tennessee.)

Three hundred bushwhackers were to have assembled where we halted; but for some cause not more than fifty reported at the "Rock-House." Among those who did report were three old fellow prisoners, who escaped the same day that we did. They came in company with some bushwhackers, each one having a gun and plenty of ammunition.

I only remember the names of two of the gentlemen, Captain Wilson, I think of the 147th New York Volunteers, and Lieutenant Telford of the 45th New York Volunteers.

There were not enough of us to assault the rebel camp, some six miles from where we were. We contented ourselves with skirmishing. After the skirmish, we again started on our route; this time with a large party, and all armed. From this time untill we got to Knoxville we marched in daylight.

I cannot pass by the Crab-Orchard, Tennessee, however, without saying that I spent in it one of the most pleasant days of my life They were all Union people, and treated us in the most hospitable manner.

We started from Charlotte, North Carolina, on the 17th day of February and arrived in Knoxville, Tennessee, on the 17th day of March, 1865. It was the happiest day of my life.

From the routes we had to take we must have walked at least five hundred miles, and in the worst kind of weather. For half the distance I had no shoes, and was most of the time hungry and cold. This too after an imprisonment of nineteen months, in the hands of a barbarous, worse than barbarous, enemy, whose chief delight was to starve prisoners. But it is past. Right is triumphant, and I will be content if the leading scoundrels are hung. Wirz is a monster, but Tabb, Semple, the two Turners and others are just as bad.

    Respectfully Yours,
     DANIEL B MEANY,
      Late Captain 13th Pa. Cavalry.

About one mile from our camp were quartered a few hundred of our soldiers who had taken the oath of allegiance in the various Southern pens, in order to save their lives. I conversed with many of them, and three or four officers found men of their command among them. They all told the same story—that they were naked, hungry and dying, and were forced to take the oath to preserve their lives; that they never could be made to fight against the United States; that their hate for rebels was still the same, and their love for the old flag could only cease with their deaths. They said one hundred and fifty had left camp the previous week to try and reach our lines; that they were leaving every day; that they had never been armed, and the rebels would not trust them; that when they first got out of prison a few were armed, but they had gone to their old companions and taken their arms with them.

  At Charlotte the excitement about exchange

grew intense. Nearly every prisoner in camp had it "on the brain," nor could they sleep day or night. The more the incredulous reflected on the great topic, they would become the more excited and lively, then they would slowly utter such sentences as: "There may be something in it;" "It might be so." There had previously been so many rumors of exchange, which generally emanated from some excited brain, and ended, as it began, in talk, that it was some time before credit was given to the report, and then only when the rolls came to be signed which paroled us. The following is a copy of the parole we signed:

> We, the undersigned, prisoners of war, do give our parole of honor that we will not take up arms again, nor serve as military police, or constabulary force, in any fort, army, garrison or field-work, nor as guards of prisoners, depots and stores, nor to discharge any duty usually performed by soldiers, until exchanged under the cartel entered into July 22nd, 1862.—And we also pledge ourselves not to communicate any information in our possession to our Government or others.

All left Charlotte with merry hearts, only a few rebel soldiers accompanying us, rejoicing in the thought of seeing home and dear friends soon. At Greensboro we took the Wilmington and Danville road for Raleigh. At Gibsonville station the truck of the car I was on broke down, and very nearly resulted in a serious accident. One end of the car had been dragged for hundreds of yards, and it was only through Divine interposition our lives were spared. We were detained here twenty-four hours, and as we were homeward bound, every hour seemed to be a month. As we were no longer surrounded by savage guards, all got out of the car and stretched their limbs in pacing around the station. I visited several families and had a long talk with them. They professed to be Union people and said they had been opposed to secession. One lady, sobbing, and stifling her tears as best she could, told me her husband had been a Union man; that he was conscripted and deserted, but was caught near our lines and tried by court-martial and shot.

> "O liberty! heav'n's choice prerogative!
> True land of law! thou social soul of property!
> Thou breath of reason! life of life itself!
> For thee the valiant bleed! O sacred liberty!
> Wing'd from the summer's snare, from flattering ruin,
> Like the bold stork you see the wintry shore,
> Leave courts, and pomps, and palaces to slaves,
> Cleave to the cold, and rest upon the storm."

Whilst stopping at the station, a crowd of rabid secessionists congregated around our car, and desiring to know what traitors thought of Northern copperheads, I said to one of the most violent:

"You rebels have sympathizers in the North."

Pucking up his mouth, and emptying it of a

stream of tobacco juice, he answered: "Wall; there be ab'lition Yankees among we 'uns; but they'se made fight and thar talk ain't of any account."

"But what do you think of copperheads?"

"Wall; I has always said my niggers has'nt souls, but I thinks they'd fight; but them 'uns North won't fight; and if there be any in the States that has'nt souls, they are'nt niggers, but *copperheads!*"

Such were the words of a Southern rebel.

After one day's detention, and getting a new truck, we again started and arrived in Raleigh, a large town and capital of the State. We lay around the depot all day, and in the evening were sent to Camp Holmes, some three miles from the city. The camp was regularly laid out, with log-houses erected for officers' quarters and men's barracks, company streets and a parade ground. At this time Fort Fisher and the City of Wilmington fell into the hands of the Union troops, and the greatest fear and consternation prevailed throughout eastern North Carolina. On all sides they were menaced; a division of cavalry was marching from the West; Sherman's brave and amphibious host was advancing from the South, swimming streams and wading swamps and completely "cleaning out" the armed but demoralized traitors; whilst the conquerors of Fort Fisher were triumphantly pushing from the east. The boasting rebels acknowledged they were whipped—that they were in the "last ditch," but could not see that it would be bravery or policy for them to die there.

A man connected with a newspaper, the Raleigh *Progress*, come into camp and made an address against the rebel authorities, to the amusement of a crowd of officers. He said, "he had always been a Union man, and had opposed from the beginning the war waged by traitors against the United States flag; he thanked God the day had arrived for their overthrow; that the time had come when he could speak his sentiments." But that good time had not quite come, for a rebel guard stopped his speech and forcibly put him out of camp.

Officers under a parole are not guarded. The parole binds them as gentlemen to remain neutral. Had the hundreds of officers who stopped for a few days at Raleigh not been paroled, they could have captured the city, and could probably have held it until the force advancing from the east came to their assistance. One day a few of the prisoners found their way into the city, and strolled through it and returned to camp. The next day several of the newspapers published leading editorials commenting on the barbarity of Yankee vandals. One advocated our close confinement, together with all the negroes, before the city would be captured and all the old men and children put to the sword, and the women carried into worse than heathen captivity. It was laughable to read the ravings of the rebel braggarts.

I visited a family of "snuff-dippers" by the name of Black. The parents and five daughters were at home, and two sons in the army. All the girls were inveterate "dippers." The process of "dipping" was in the following style: Each dipper had a small cup of snuff, with two sticks in it about three inches long, with a rag wrapped on the end of each stick; these were dipped in the snuff and one placed in the side of each jaw; the sticks protruding from the mouth and crossing each other, resembling the letter x. Putting on a *Southern* air they would gabble like geese, with the sticks in their mouths. One said to me, enjoying her "dipping:"

"You'uns can't whip we'uns; we'uns fight and you'uns don't; we'uns have the old stock blud; we'uns like our niggers and you'uns don't."

I thought they did love their negroes beyond the bounds of decency, and that the blood in their veins was of a *very old stock*.

February 27th we left Raleigh and arrived at Goldsborough at twelve o'clock, a. m., next day. All along the route the people were excited, and it was evident to the most careless observer that they no longer had any faith in their bad cause. At Goldsborough they were not only excited, but were afraid of being punished by the soldiers of the Union for their wicked and villainous acts of the previous four years. We went into camp alongside of the railroad, three miles from the town.

Three-quarters of a mile from our camp were a few hundred of our enlisted men. They were all sick, naked, hungry and dying. I visited the camp, and during the short time I remained at it, three of the poor fellows died. In place of the rebels sending the unwell men through the lines, they sent the healthy, (though none were well, and two-thirds would surely die,) and allowed the sickly to lie out in a field without any covering whatever, and gave them no food, to die of neglect, want and starvation. The officers, and they were poorly clad, almost stripped themselves of their lousy rags to clothe the poor and unfortunate men, and hide their nakedness. They were all but the shadows of men, and as black as negroes with dirty pine smoke. I helped to wash several of the poor fellows, and found it impossible to get the dirt off; it was ground into the flesh. The little flesh on many of them presented a disgusting appearance from the effects of vermin. They were a horrible, pitiful sight. As I gazed on their skeleton forms, their ghastly looks and emaciated figures, I articulated a prayer, sat down and cried, and then I resolved, whilst God spared my life, that my voice and pen would be devoted on all occasions to show to my Northern fellow citizens the dreadful atrocities perpetrated by Southern fiends on helpless men.

"The tyrannous and bloody act is done ;
The most arch deed of piteous massacre,
That ever yet this land was guilty of."

I had a talk with a Union family by the name of Robinson, a few hundred yards from the camp. The husband was in our lines. He had been dragged from his home and put into the rebel army; a few days afterwards he deserted. They gave me a supply of bacon and bread. They made soup for the enlisted men; but the brutal commander of the guard cursed them and would not allow them to take it in to the poor fellows, who were crying for bread and water.

We left Goldsborough on the evening of February 28th and arrived at East Bridge, the place of exchange, on March 1st, and at 9 o'clock, a m, passed through a guard of our own troops—who presented arms to us—into the Federal lines. Every man said it was the happiest day of his life; and although we cried for joy, we did not forget our murdered companions whom we left behind, and could say with the poet:

> "Give me the death of those
>   Who for their country die,
> And oh! be mine like their repose,
>   When cold and low they lie.
> Their loveliest mother earth
>   Enshrines the fallen brave;
> In her sweet lap who gave them birth,
>   They find their tranquil grave."

CHAPTER XIX.

"Up From the Valley of Death"—The Reception Given to Us.—Plenty to Eat and Gladness of Heart—Wilmington—Annapolis—Skeletons Among Their Friends—Altered Appearance of Officers—Honorably Discharged—Home—Let Us Have Justice.

> "Maker! Preserver! my Redeemer! God!
> Whom have I in the heavens but thee alone?
> On earth but Thee, whom should I praise, whom love?
> For thou hast brought me hitherto, upheld
> By thy omnipotence; and from thy grace,
> Unbought, unmerited, though not unsought;—
> The wells of my salvation hast refresh'd
> My spirit, watering it at morn and eve."

If any of my readers have ever been in foreign lands, and had not heard from the dear ones at home for years, and returned, and when about to open the door to know the worst or the best, they can remember the occurrence with peculiar feelings of satisfaction and joy;—or if they have ever been in a desperate battle where nearly all their companions were killed, and they, as if by a miracle, were spared; or if they have ever been engaged in any fearful enterprise where they were wonderfully preserved, they can remember, whilst they live, the moment they were out of danger and raised from a threatened death to a sure life; or if any of my readers have ever been marvelously delivered from a shipwreck, a boiler explosion, or an awful accident on a rail-road, they can imagine what our feelings were when we were again under the stars and stripes—when we were once more with our old companions in arms, and out of the hands of not only a brutal enemy but fiends; again, as many of the captives irreverently expressed it, "In God's Country!"

Colonel Mulford and his staff were the first Union officers of whom we caught a glimpse, and no sooner were they observed than they received three of the heartiest cheers ever given by one thousand United States officers. Colonel Hatch, the Rebel Commissioner of Exchange, and Colonel Mulford, the Federal Commissioner, counted us as we passed through the ranks of our soldiers, at an open order, faced inward, with their arms at a present. As each one reached the outer file, he started on a double-quick, shouting, whooping, hallooing, alternately crying and laughing, and running like a wild man. Some jumped as high as they could; others ran down the road for a quarter of a mile, throwing away everything they possessed; many rolled on the ground, cheering, shouting and hugging each other, shaking hands and crying like children, giving way to the wildest fits of joy in which human nature ever engaged. Those who had bags of corn-meal, untied the mouths of their sacks and threw the coarse stuff over their companions. Pots, skillets, griddles, bundles of rags, worthless articles, loads of trash and lousy clothing were now thrown away—a few hours previous they were of intrinsic value. All felt they were in a land of plenty and among civilized beings, and would find clothing to hide their nakedness and food to prevent starvation.

We walked about a mile and a quarter from the place of exchange, along a road picketed by our troops, singing and feeling gay, and thinking, as we looked upon the bright uniforms and manly forms of our boys, that we were among men and not ragamuffins and butchers. Suddenly turning a bend in the road, "Old Glory," the Stars and Stripes, for the first time, greeted our eyes. A deafening cheer went up from the head of the column, which was caught up and repeated by every voice along its entire length. Again and again every man cheered, until he was entirely exhausted and hoarse. All felt that it was the greatest day of their lives. The Sixth Connecticut Volunteer Infantry were in camp on the north side of the Cape Fear River, and on a small hill, at a respectable distance where all could see, they had erected a beautiful arbor of evergreens, and from its center hung their colors, whilst an arch surrounded a placard, on which was painted the touching words: "WELCOME, BROTHERS!" The splendid band of the regiment played "Hail to the Chief," as we marched past it with uncovered heads and hearts filled with gratitude to the Great Ruler of the Universe for our restoration to friends. The whole division turned out to welcome us in their holiday attire; a grand and pleasing sight to us, who had been so long the prisoners of rebel vagabonds. The troops were drawn up in line, with ranks opened the width of the road, faced inwards. We passed through them, receiving congratulations and sympathizing words. Each regiment had its flag, for which, as the officers passed, they gave three cheers. The old prisoners stepped out of the ranks, and, as their eyes filled with tears, hugged and kissed the flag of their country—embraced their old and endeared friend from whom they had so long been parted.

After a short walk, we were conducted to a delightful piece of woods, where there was an abundant supply of Uncle Sam's substantial food, such as bread, boiled fresh beef and coffee. Only those who have been nearly starved can imagine our enjoyment of a full stomach. After music, singing and dancing, we walked a few miles to Wilmington, North Carolina, where we took steamers for Annapolis, Maryland. It was a rough passage for all of us, who were not in the best of health, and all were sea sick; but, through the gentlemanly and executive abilities of Colonel Thorp and a few other officers, who made milk punch, cooked coffee, etc., the sea voyage was rendered tolerably comfortable. Thousands of our enlisted men, who had been prisoners, were in Camp Parole, Annapolis, Maryland. Daily dozens died. It was common to see fifteen or twenty corpses at one funeral. I saw one man walk overboard; the poor fellow's mind was gone; he did not know what he was doing. I talked to several of the unfortunate men, but could get nothing out of them; they would stare at me, and were so far gone that they did not know their own name or the regiment to which they belonged. How many thousands of the following kind of obituary notices were published in the different papers throughout the country during last spring and summer!

JOSEPH H. PRITCHET, late of No. 848 N. Twelfth Street, Philadelphia, and a member of Company C, Seventy-second Regiment Pennsylvania Volunteers, Colonel Baxter's Fire Zouaves; from the effects of brutal treatment and starvation at Andersonville, Georgia.

Storekeepers at Annapolis gave us trust, but next day all the officers received part of their pay and settled their bills. Barber shops, clothing and shoe stores were besieged. Officers cleanly shaved, or with some peculiar style of whiskers, would go into clothing stores, select a complete outfit, (never asking the price) throw away their lousy rags, don their suits, and walk into the street, so completely altered in appearance that their old and most intimate prison companions *could not recognize them.*

At Annapolis those whose term of service had not expired, received thirty days furlough to visit their homes, and those whose had were honorably discharged, *from the date of the order mustering them out,* which was the beginning of March, 1865.

About the first of March I heard from my home for the first time in nearly one year. Although boxes were sent me, and letters every few weeks, I never received them. I could not tell whether my people knew I was living or dead. When I visited home, my readers can imagine the joyful meeting!

The war is over. Right has triumphed over Wrong! All hearts have rejoiced. Let us not, as a people, fail to give always the honor and glory of our success to the Great Commander in the heavens. Let Wirz, Tabb, Sedden, Davis, and all the murderers of our prisoners, from the highest to the lowest, feel the punishment which they deserve, for committing such a *cruel* wrong, and the people, especially those who have been soldiers, will rest satisfied.

> "Great God! we thank thee for this home,
>   This bounteous birthland of the free;
> Where wanderers from afar may come,
>   And breathe the air of liberty!—
> Still may her flowers untrampled spring,
>   Her harvests wave, her cities rise;
> And yet, till Time shall fold his wing,
>   Remain Earth's loveliest Paradise!"

APPENDIX.

ROLL OF HONOR.

NAMES

OF

The Pennsylvania Soldiers who died at Andersonville,

FROM THE EFFECTS OF

BRUTAL TREATMENT AND STARVATION!

> "Each soldier's name
> Shall shine untarnish'd on the rolls of fame,
> And stand the example of each distant age,
> And add new lustre to the historic page!"

From the time Governor Curtin was convinced of the fact that the Soldiers of the Union were being starved, and dying by thousands in Southern prisons, he has been engaged in procuring some data by which he could ascertain the names of those who perished. He met with success; and now, through the courtesy of Colonel Joseph Phillips, Surgeon-General of Pennsylvania, a correspondent of the Philadelphia PRESS secured a full and complete list of Pennsylvania soldiers, who died at the rebel prisons at Andersonville, Georgia, from February 26th, 1864, to March 24th, 1865, with the regiment to which each belonged, and date of death.

A copy of the original list of their names was furnished to Governor Curtin by Thomas C. Tripler, lieutenant and adjutant 39th Infantry Missouri Volunteers and adjutant of paroled men at Benton Barracks, St. Louis. The list came into Adjutant Tripler's possession through Charles Lang, hospital steward of the 101st Regiment Pennsylvania Volunteers, who was captured at Plymouth, North Carolina. This patient and considerate soldier preserved a record of the names of such of his comrades as perished while he was at Andersonville, and copied from the records of the prison itself such other names as he could gather, and now we have the result of his forethought and labor in the list herewith published. He surely deserves, as he will receive, the grateful thanks of those in Pennsylvania whose sons and husbands and fathers and brothers perished at Andersonville.

ROLL OF HONOR.

The following is a CORRECT *List, with the name and regiment to which each belonged, and the date of death.*

Atwood, A, 18, Mh. 29, '64
Armidster, M, 4, Mh. 30,'64
Acherman C, 28, Ap. 10, '64
Arb, S, 4, Ap. 27, '64
Allgut, H, 54, May 9, '64
Akers, G.K, 90, June 23, '64
Allison, E, 55, June 24, '64
Anderson, D, 103, June 27, '64
Able, J, 54, June 29, '64
Amugast, E, 103, July 6, '64
Ackley, G. B, 3, July 8, '64
Alexander M, 1, July 14, '64
Andray, J. T, 13, July 25, '64
Anderson, J, 79, July 27, '64
Aches, F. J, 7, July 28, '64
Alcorn, G. W. 143, July 28, '64
Archit, H, 55, July 29, '64
Allen, C, 8, Aug. 4, '64,
Anderson, J, 8, Aug. 7, '64
Aler, B, 103, Aug. 11, '64
Auft, J, 101, Aug. 13, '64
Armstrong, P, 4, Aug. 16, '64
Ahorson, J, 91, Aug. 18, '64
Arnold, D, 184, Aug. 29, '64
Augstedt, G, 1, Sept. 5, '64
Aller, J. L, 101, Sept. 7, '64
Ambler, C, 13, Sept. 9, '64
Alexander, W, 2, Sept. 10, '64
Armstrong, H, 7, Sep. 13, '64
Arnold, L, 73, Sep. 13, '64
Altemus, W, 7, Sep. 14, '64
Alcom, J, 18. Sep. 18, '64
Allison, D. B, 55, Sep. 27, '64
Anderson, A, 135, Oc. 7, '64
Allen, D, 126, Oc. 9, '64
Alten, T, 7, Oc. 13, '64
Appleby, J, 149, Oc. 24, '64
Antill, J, 61, Oc. 28, '64
Angen, W, 118, Nov. 1, '64

Afflerb, T, 2. Nov. 6, '64
Atchison, W, 142, Jan. 25, '65
Arnos, J, Art. May 5, '64
Ball, F, 4, March 29, '64
Burton, L, 18, Mh. 30, '64
Briggs, A, 13, Ap. 3, '64
Beugler, A, 27, Ap. 8, '64
Breel, J, 27, Ap. 14, '64
Black, J, 14, Ap. 15, '64
Bradley, A, 3, Ap. 21, '64
Burns, S, 73, Ap. 22, '64
Barr, A. J, 54, Ap. 22, '64
Bayne, W, 145, May 1, '64
Bradley, M, 3, May 4, '64
Brown, H, 90, May 5, '64
Brown, D, 4, May 7, '64
Batting, I. 8, May 9, '64
Berkhamer, H, 73, June 12, '64
Brooks, D, 79, June 12, '64
Brian, C, 183, June 14, '64
Byter, P, 73, June 15, '64
Burns, O, 13, June 16, '64
Bigler, M, 4, June 16, '64
Brown, C, 3, June 17, '64
Buckhannah, W, 3, June 18, '64
Ball, L, 26, June 19, '64
Barr, J. S, 4, June 20, '64
Baker, H, 18, June 22, '64
Bissell, J, 18, June 26, '64
Balsley, W, 20, June 26, '64
Brown, M, 14, June 28, '64
Bruen, J, 73, July 1, '64
Bolt, H, J, 18, July 1, '64
Beane, J, 76, July 1, '64
Burns, J, 13, July 3, '64
Bish, J, 103, July 5, '64
Brien, J, 56, July 5, '64

Belford, J, 145, July 5, '64
Bryan, P, 3, July 7, '64
Barr, S, 103, July 8, '64
Brenny, J, 48, July 8, '64
Barnes, W, 101, July 8, '64
Butler, L, 118, July, '64
Brunt, A, 119, July 10, '64
Burdeni, A, 119, July 10, '64
Beard, O, 54 July 13, 64
Burns, J, 103, July 14, '64
Brinton, J, 157, July 17, '64
Baker, W, 103, July 17, '64
Burnside, J, 57, July 18, '64
Bluch, W, 103, July 19, '64
Billing, J, 13, July 21, '64
Brelinger, W. R, 4, July 21, '64
Buttler, C. P. 148, July 22, '64
Batchel, D, 55, July 23, '64
Bright, E, 90, July 24, '64
Bradford, L, 10, July 26, '64
Berkley, M, 50, July 26, '64
Balkner, A, 116, July 27, '64
Barrett, I, 6, July 29, '64
Brown, J, 53, July 31, '64
Butler, D, 53, July 31, '64
Barry, S, 77, July 31, '64
Barton, J, 4, Aug. 1, '64
Burke, J, 90, Aug. 1, '64
Bernheart, F, 12, Aug 2, '64
Baker, E, 4, Aug. 3, '64
Behres, A, 73, Aug. 4, '64
Benethes, G, 55, Aug. 5, '64
Bowers, J, 2, Aug. 7, '64
Bumgratte, C, 73. Aug. 8, '64
Barger, C, 6, Aug. 8, '64
Buck, B F, 2, Aug. 8, '64
Brown, M, 50, Aug. 9, '64
Burlingame, A J, 141, Aug. 11, '64
Bear, J, 79, Aug. 12, '64
Bruce, J, 101, Aug. 12, '64
Bower, B, 6, Aug. 12, '64
Brougham, H, 143, Aug. 14, '64
Buck, B F, 2, Aug. 14, '64
Browning, F, 103, Aug. 16, '64
Boughanberger, A, 115, Aug 17, '64
Boyer F, , 43, Aug. 17, '64
Baker, J, 101, Aug. 18, '64
Bower, G N, 103, Aug. 18, '64
Bailey G F, 18, Aug. 18, '64
Bertrand, J A, 103, Aug. 19, '64
Bear, S, 55, Aug. 20, '64
Boles, M S, 4, Aug. 20, '64
Bowers, C, 101, Aug. 20, '64
Briney, J, 4, Aug. 20, '64
Burddick, L, 148, Aug. 21, '64
Bennett, A, 67, Aug. 22, '64
Blackman, A, 18, Aug. 22, '64
Brannon, P, 7, Aug. 22, '64
Baldwin, A, 5, Aug. 23, '64
Barrett, E F, 149, Aug. 23, '64
Bell, T, 11, Aug. 23, '64
Bare, J G, 46, Aug. 24, '64
Breckenridge, N, 73, Aug. 24, '64
Bowman, A, 63, Aug. 24, '64
Boyd, J, 101, Aug. 24, '64
Benner W, 145, Aug. 24, '64
Brittingham, J, 20, Aug. 25, '64
Bangarden, J, 149, Aug. 25, '64
Bown, F, 11, Ang. 26, '64
Brayan, L, 106, Aug. 26, '64
Bridaham, A W, 55, Aug. 28, '64
Berner, S, 184, Aug. 29, '64
Ball, P, 49, Aug. 31, '64
Barner, W, 119, Sep. 1, '64
Bennet', J, 55, Sep. 1, '64

Barnett, M, 145, Sep. 2, '64
Black, J, 143, Sep. 3, '64
Blair, J G, 49, Sep. 3, '64
Brink, F, 11, Sep. 4, '64
Browne, J, 184, Sep. 5, '64
Brinley, F, 54, Sep. 6, '64
Bright, A, 101, Sep. 7, '64
Boland, D, 183, Sep. 7, '64
Barr, P, 103, Sep. 9, '64
Brown, L, 8, Sep. 9, '64
Brown, A, 101, Sep. 10, '64
Brickerstaff, W, 101, Sep. 10, '64
Bruce, B. 101, Sep. 10, '64
Blassar, J, 7, Sep. 11, '64
Bousteak, T D, 106, Sep. 11, '64
Bichert. E, 57, Sep. 11, '64
Bootz, E. B. 57, Sep. 11, '64
Baughman, G, 138, Sep. 13, '64
Beattie, R, 95, Sep. 14, '64
Boyer, J M, 7, Sep. 14, '64
Bentley, S, 54, Sep. 14. '64
Brown, P, 55, Sep. 15, '64
Baker, J, 7, Sep. 16. '64
Blake, E, 69, Sep. 18, '64
Boylen, J, 7, Sep. 22, '64
Baldwin, A, 51, Sep. 24, '64
Bowers, F, 5, Sep. 25, '64
Bowewell, W, 14, Sep. 26, '64
Blair, G, 7, Sep. 28, '64
Burdge, L H, 3, Oct. 2, '64
Byers, S, 22, Oct. 2, '64
Burns, J, 103, Oct. 2, '64
Brown, G, 10, Oct. 4, '64
Burgess, H, 27, Oct. 5, '64
Buck, D C, 2, Oct. 8, '64
Billinger, G, 87, Oct. 9, '64
Blackman, W, 184, Oct. 11, '64
Brightel. T, 51, Oct. 11, '64
Bois, J M, 143, Oct. 12, '64
Bowling, J, 3, Oct. 12, '64
Bartheart, J, 116, Oct. 15, '64
Barney, G, 4, Oct. 15, '64
Banyar, J, 55, Oct. 15, '64
Bunker, T, 55, Oct. 15, '64
Bowman, G, 49, Oct. 17. '64
Bisil, B, 142, Oct. 22, '64
Bruce, H, 11, Oct. 23, '64
Burks, G, 51, Oct. 24, '64
Ball, J, 19, Oct. 25, '64
Bain, G, 183, Oct. 26, '64
Baney, -, 4, Oct. 26, '64
Baker, B W, 142, Oct. 26, '64
Brack, C, 46, Oct. 27, '64
Berghtley, W, 103, Oct. 27, '64
Blain, J, 106, Oct. 28, '64
Boyer, T, 11, Oct. 29, '64
Burr, E, 145, Oct. 29, '64
Ballinger, G, 87, Oct. 30, '64
Burch, H, 2, Nov. 7, '64
Burke, J, 22, Nov. 8, '64
Bupp, L, 149, Nov. 12, '64
Bailey, J, 2, Nov. 16, '64
Bogar, D, 184 Nov. 18, '64
Bond, C C, 20, Nov. 18, '64
Brady, H, 5, Nov. 19, '64
Blubaker, B P, 79, Nov. 26, '64
Braddock, T, 77, Nov. 27, '64
Burrows, J, 5, Jan. 9, '65
Burnett, J, 184, Feb, 27, '65
Barnett, J, 184, Feb. 27, '65
Carter, W, 139, Mch. 14, '64
Chase, W, 13, Mch. 22, '64
Christian, G, 54, Mch. 23, '64
Campsey, J, 16, Mch. 25, '64
Carmard, F, 54, Ap. 4 '64
Coyle, P, 45, Ap. 9, '64
Crouch, L, 4, Ap. 10, '64

Croughan, J, 3, Ap. 11, '64
Case, D, 8, Ap. 14, '64
Camer, A, 4, Ap. 25, '64
Cravener, S, 14, May 1, '64
Curry, A, 119, May 3, '64
Campbell, W, 8, May 10, '64
Charter, W, 101, June 11, '64
Calvert, R P, 6, June 11, '64
Coombs, J, 3, June 12, '64
Coy, J A, 13, June 12, '64
Culbertson, J, 13, June 14, '64
Cooper, F. 18, June 16. '64
Carry, R, 73, June 16, '64
Coyle, H, 81, June 24, '64
Crouse, E, 141, June 25, '64
Copple, F, 54, June 30, '64
Chapman, J, 7, July 6, '64
Cannon, J, 4, July 4, '64
Caban, S, 103, July 4, '64
Coleman, J, 18, July 7, '64
Chase, S, 72, July 14, '64
Clark, H, 8, July 16, '64
Caton, W, 49, July 16, '64
Couch, B, 50, July 17, '64
Coyle, E, 58, July 24, '64
Curty, L, 2, July 26, '64
Carpenter, L, 12, July 27, '64
Cautrell, M, 6, July 28, '64
Cinklin, A. 90. July 29, '64
Chapman, P, 3, July 30, '64
Crawford. M, 14, July 31, '64
Cox, J, 103, July 31, '64
Claybaugh, G W, 7, Jul 31, '64
Crock, H, 45, Aug. 1. '64
Croup, U, 104, Aug. 4, '64
Cochrane, C, 103, Aug. 4, '64
Chew, J, 18, Aug. 6, '64
Cramer, E. 4, Aug. 9, '64
Campbell, J, 13, Aug. 11, '64
Cregg, J G, 54, Aug. 12, '64
Cumberland, T, 14, Aug. 12, '64

Connahan, M, 115, Aug. 13, '64
Carpenter, W C, 115, Aug. 14, '64
Campbell, R D, 11, Aug. 14, '64
Cox, H, 7, Aug. 14, '64
Cummings, B, 3, Aug. 16, '64
Coriner, J, 184, Aug. 17, '64
Corbin, W, 49, Aug. 20, '64
Campbell, R, 11, Aug. 20, '64
Coon, G, 2, Aug. 21, '64
Cameron, W, 101, Aug. 21, '64
Connelly, W, 55, Aug. 22, '64
Conner, J, 6, Aug. 22, '64
Cline, T, 3, Aug. 22, '64
Crawford, J, 77, Aug. 23, '64
Coleman, C, 19, Aug. 23, '64
Comly, J, 101, Aug. 24, '64
Craft, A, 90, Aug. 26, '64
Cobert, F, 11, Aug. 27, '64
Carr, J, 51, Aug. 28, '64
Cathcart, R, 103, Aug. 29, '64
Cram, J, 4, Aug. 29, '64
Creig, W, 103, Sept. 1, '64.
Clay, H, 184, Sept. 1, '64
Curry, S, 140, Sept. 2, '64.
Carroll, A, 2, Sept 2, '64.
Campbell, G. T, 93, Sept. 3, '64.
Criser, M, 54, Sept. 3, '64.
Crawford, J. A, 103, Sept. 8, '64.
Collins, M, 101, Sep. 8, '64
Cole, J. C, 118, Sept. 8, '64
Chapman, G, 18, Sep. 19, '64
Coyle, M, 79, Sept. 12, '64
Culvet, J, 69, Sept. 12, '64
Cluster, 11, Sept. 13, '64.

Cavender, J. L, 149, Sept. 14, '64.
Cysey, A, 3, Sept. 16, '64
Coffman, W, 15, Sept. 18, '64
Cramer, E, 55, Sept. 18, '64
Church, C. H, 45, Sep. 18, '64
Clark, J, 101, Sept. 19, '64
Carney, J. J, 149, Sept. 19, '64
Coats, S. B. 135, Sept. 20, '64
Comptz, S, 1, Sept. 21, '64
Crum, O, 149, Sept. 23, '64
Cline, J, 118, Sept. 24, '64
Carleton, G, 45, Sept. 26, '64
Cummings, R. 65, Sept. 27, '64
Callahan, M, 52, Sept. 27, '64
Conrod, W, 14, Sept. 28, '64
Campbell, W, 13, Sept. 30, '64
Coats, S. R, 139, Oct. 1, '64
Crawford, G, 1, Oct. 2, '64
Canton, L, 13, Oct. 2, '64
Cromicle, F, 7, Oct. 4, '64
Cornelius W, 4, Oct. 5, '64
Cullingford, R, 7, Oct. 6, '64
Caldwell, R, 7, Oct. 6, '64
Clark, W, 5, Oct. 7, '64
Canby, G. C, 2, Oct. 7, '64
Coferhaven, W. 1, Oct. 8, '64
Culbertson, L, 75, Oct. 8, '64
Corbin, M, 184, Oct. 13, '64
Clark, S, 1, Oct. 13, '64
Coe, Geo, 145, Oct. 16, '64
Clach, J, 3, Oct. 16, '64
Clark, H, 184, Oct. 21, '64
Clark, E. B, 101, Oct. 22, '64
Card, W, 145, Oct. 23, '64
Crawford, L, 184, Oct. 24, '64
Cole, H. O, 2, Oct. 24, 64
Campbell, C. A, 11, Oct. 26, '64
Creagan, G, 1, Oct. 27, '64
Crawford, M, 14, Oct. 29, '64
Cramer, G, 116, Oct. 30, '64
Coffin, H, 54, Oct. 30, '64
Crawley, G, 20, Oct. 30, '64

Cragger, W. H, 5, Nov. 4, 64
Chacen, A. W, 106, Nov. 4, '64
Colebaugh, W, 60, Nov. 5, '64
Crandall, A. 145, Nov. 6, '64
Cleveland, E, 18, Nov. 8, '64
Crampton, A. B, 143, Nov. 13, '64
Cullen, T. P, 31, Nov. 22, '64
Cornoay, C, 2, Nov. 23, '64
Compton, F. G, 71, Dec. 10, '64
Cone, S, 115, Dec. 16, '64
Culp, P. K, 138, Dec. 17, '64
Connor, Z, 112, Jan. 1, '65
Clark, J, 89, Jan. 10, '65
Collins, G, 118, Jan. 19, '65
Cassel, D, 20, Feb 4, '65
Clarke, F. D, 7, Feb. 20, '65
Campbell, D, art. Mar. 20, '65
Collins, H, 88, July 11, '65
Davidson, H, 57, Mar. 25, '64
Dow, Thos, 119, Mar. 3, '64
Dun, R. B, 101, June 29, '64
Donovan, I, 139, June 29, '64
Deiley, Wm, 53, July 1, '64
Davis, M, 22, July 26, '64
Daton, C. 8, July 9, '64
Degert, H, 15, July 15, '64
Davidson, C, 100, July 15, '64
Dalton, Jas, 8, July 21, '64
Davis, Jas, 103, July 22, '64
Dawes, M. M, 103, July 24, '64
Dougherty, J, 7, July 26, '64
Devon, R. P, 149, July 27, '64
Drinkle, J. A, 79, July 29, '64
Dechman, J, 184, July 29, '64
Dodrick, L, 50, Aug. 1, '64
Denton, M, 9, Aug. 1, '64
Day, Wm, 97, Aug. 1, '64
Davis, J, 101, Aug. 3, '64
Dort, C. W, 4, Aug. 4, '64
Dondle, R, 101, Aug. 5, '64
Davy, H, 68, Aug. 5, '64
Darenbrook, J, 101, Aug. 5, '64

Dalancy, J, 101, Aug. 6, '64
Dunbar, John, 14, Aug. 6, '64
Deacon, J, 148, Aug. 6, '64
Dawlin, L, 110, Aug. 8, '64
Ditz'el, L, 73, Aug. 10, '64
Dandson, G, 57, Aug. 12, '64
Dougherty, 101, Aug. 12, '64
Decker, J, 45, Aug. 14, '64
Day, A. H, 2, Aug. 15, '64
Doran, P, 99, Aug. 15, '64
Deal, F, 63, Aug. 17, '64
Degrott. H, 13, Aug. 18, '64
Defree, Jas, 15, Aug. 19, '64
Dodge, A, 18, Aug. 20, '64
Davis, Wm, 103, Aug. 20 '64
Dawney, G, 148, Aug. 23, '64
Donovan, D, 90, Aug. 23, '64
Dunn, John, 69, Aug. 23, '64
Dakenfelt, J, 55, Aug. 28, '64
Day, S, 13, Aug. 30, '64
Dively, J, 119, Aug. 31, '64
Dilkes, C, 1, Sept. 1, '64
Deivill, S, 50, Sep'. 3, '64.
Dougherty, G. R, 184, Sep. 4, '64
Dixon, J, 105, Sept. 7, '64
Dougherty, J, 73, Sept. 10, '64
Duff, J, 4, Sept. 12, '64.
Dougherty, F, 90, Sept. 12, '64
Durhous, B, 11, Sept. 14, '64
Donnelly, J, 97, Sept. 15, '64
Davidson, C, 90, Sept. 18, '64
Discoll, H. C. 26, Sept. 18, '64
Duffee, J, 52, Sept. 18, '64
Delaney, E, 7, Sept. 19, '64
Dort, R, 19, Sept. 21, '64
Davidson, G, 12, Sept. 29. '64
Dougherty, M, 51, Oct. 2, '64
Dukate, J, 1, Oct. 6, '64
Dalzell, J. G, 139, Oct. 14, '64
Dixon, B, 145, Oct. 20, '64
Demry, Fred, 20, Oct. 22, '64
Diehl, C, 55, Oct. 23, '64
Dermon, A, 77, Oct. 24, '64

Dewitt, M, 1, Oct. 24, '64
Davidson, S, 184, 29, '64
Davis, John, 66, Nov. 2, '6
Dickens, C, 2, Nov. 13, '643
Dalrymple, J. E, 145 Nov. 2
Dowley, P, 120, Jan. 5, '65
Deeds, J, 13, Feb. 2, '65
Deems, P, art, Ap. 26, '64
Delaney, I, 83, July 11, '65
Etters, H, 13, May 9, '64
Elliott, J, 13, June 17, '64
Elliott, J, 69, July 2, '64
Erwin, C, 7, July 8, '64.
Espy, J, 145, July 9, '64
Elliott, J. P, 10, July 14, '64
Elright, B, 9, July 23, '64
Eaton, N, 1, July 30, '64
Elenberger, P, 145, Aug. 5, '64
Eby Van B, 7, Aug. 12, '64
Ennis, A, Aug. 15, '64
Errets, J, 103, Aug. 22, '64
Ellis, S, 53, Aug. 23, '64
Eccles, G, 77, Aug. 26, '64
Eusley, C, 184, Aug. 26, '64
Ellis, H. H, 18, Aug. 30, '64
Egan, John, 55, Sept. 3, '64
Eyline, Jacob, 55, Sept. 7, '64
Eichnor, C, 143, Sept. 12, '64
Earlman, J, 7, Sept. 16, '64
English, J. C, 100, Sept. 22, '64
Elfry, B. S, 7, Sept. 29, '64
Elliott, J. H, 83, Oct. 11, '64
Erdibauch, C, 3, Oct. 11, '64
Eringfelts, J, 189, Oct. 12, '64
Edgar, W. H, 7, Nov. 5, '64
Eidebence, J, 5, Nov. 5, '64
Etters, D, 145, Nov. 14, '64
Ellis, E, 11, Feb. 3, '65
Bbharts, J, 87, Feb. 18, '65
Fleehr, J, 73, Mar. 28, '64
Fick, John, 83, Apr. 12, '64
Folan, B, 13, Apr. 28, '64
Fuller, H, 13, May 10, '64

Freeman, W.M, 3, June 14, '64.
Fielton, F, 103, June 17,'64
Friday, S. D.101, June 17, 64
Fish, C. W, 101, June 18, '64
Farley, J, 54, June 18, '64
Fox, G, 78, June 20, '64
Funkhauser, J, 101, June 26, '64
Fortham, A, 50, June 26, '64
Forney, G, 13, July 4, '64
Fenriliger, E, 103, July5,'64
Ford, M, 53, July 9, 64
Frantz, J, 2, July 13, '64
Fisher, B.M, 101, July 13, '64
French, A, 2, July 19, '64
Forsythe, J, 18, July 21,'64
Feerrell, A, 12, July 22, 64
Fingley, J, 14, July 24,'64
Flick, L, 184, July 30, '64
Filey, J. H, 53, July 31, '64
Foreman, G. S, 1, Aug. 1. '64
Flyme, M, 13, Aug. 1, '64
Ferver, E, 87, Aug. 3, '64
File, C, 145, Aug. 4, '64
Fish, J, 85, Aug. 8, '64
Flemming, W, 97, Aug 9,'64
Flickinger, J, 50, Aug. 14,'64
Feney, W, 79, Aug. 15, '64
Frey, H, 4, Aug. 16, '64
Fee, Geo, 103, Aug. 16, 64
Faiss, A, 145, Aug. 18,'64
Furnam, E, 57, Aug. 19,'64
Farnen, J. S, 7, Aug. 21,'64
Fourlough, S,14,Aug.22,'64
Fox, R, 155, Aug. 23, '64
Fritzman, J. W, 18, Aug. 24, '64
Finlon, T, 143, Aug. 24, '64
Fuller, G, 2, Aug. 26, '64
Frederick, L, 148, Aug. 26, '64
French, J, 101, Aug. 26, '64
Ford, Thos, 7, Aug. 26, '64

Fullerton, E, 99, Aug. 27, '64
Foster, J, 103, Aug. 28, '64
Fisher, W, 54. Aug. 29, '64
Fry, S, 101, Aug. 29, '64
Fitzgerald, M,145,Sep.2,'64
Fahy, J, 13, Sept. 2, '64
Fritz, D, 18, Sept. 4, '64
Fullerton, J, 118, Sept.8, '64
Fetterman, J, 48, Sept.8,'64
Freeman, E.N, 9, Sept.9,'64
Francis, A, 69, Sept. 10, '64
Fagan, R, 118, Sept. 13, '64
Framce, R, 4, Sept. 15, '64
Fisher, C, 4, Sept. 17, '64
Floyd, B, 67, Sept. 18, '64
Forr, J. C, 107, Sept. 19, '64
Faish, A, 183, Sept. 27, '64
Fessenden, E. N, 149, Oct. 1, '64
Fingley, S, 14, Oct 6, '64
Fisher, W, 110, Oct. 10, '64
Flynn, S, 76, Oct. 10, '64
Free, J, 143, Oct. 11, '64
Flinn, J, 87 Oct. 11, '64
Flaeming, J, 97, Oct. 16,'64
Flamious, J, 106,Oct.18,'64
Ferguson,J.R,21,Oct.20,'64
Fox, M, 8, Oct. 23, '64
Friel, D, 55, Oct. 24, '64
Ferguson, J, 184,Oct.28,'64
Frisbee, H, 115, Nov. 2, '64
Fried, S, 53, Nov. 8, '64
Fairbanks, E, 140, Nov. 11, '64
Flagley, C, 14, Nov. 14, '64
Foust, S. L, 149, Nov.16,'64
Foster, C. W, 76, Dec. 2,'64
Falhenstein, F, 148, Dec. 8, '64
Freese, J, 52, Dec. 26, '64
Firke, J, 67, Jan. 13, '65
Faite, W. D, 20, Feb. 7, '65
Goodman, R, 13, Mar. 19,'64
Groffell, W, 73, Apr. 3, '64

Geeley, I, 145, Apr. 13, '64
Green, W, 3, Apr. 16, '64
Gorman, B, 18, May 9, '64
Greer, J.A, 13, May 10, '64
Graham, W. J, 4, May 10, '64
Gerrile, J, 19, June 13, '64
Gould, E, 73, June 14, '64
Gallegher, F, 13, June 16, '64
Gilmore, J, 110, June 17, '64
Green, A, 4, June 21, '64
Greenwold, G, 27, June 23, '64
Gumbert. A, 103, June 26, '64
Getting, J. H, 1, June 28, '64
Gross, S, 50, July 6, '64
Gotwalt, H, 55, July 6, '64
Griffin, A, 103, July 7, '64
George, A, 149, July 7, '64
Gists, H, 103, July 7, '64
Gilleland, W, 14, July 8, '64
Green, M. 26, July 12, '64
Goomch, M.A, 110, July 18, '64
Gibbs, E, 18, July 19, '64
Gregg, F, 139, July 22, '64
Glicker, J, 77, Aug. 6, '64
Gibbons, W, 11, Aug. 9, '64
Gladin, A, 21, Aug. 11, '64
Gregg, —, 139, Aug. 12, '64
Gross, J, 62, Aug. 14, '64
Gregg, D, 142, Aug. 15, '64
Graham, W, 103, Aug 15, '64
Gillespie, J, 11, Aug. 16, '64
Grouse, G. 145, Aug. 16, '64
Gettenher, D. M, 103, Aug. 16, '64
Grey, L, 163, Aug. 17, '64
Gerurd, C, 4, Aug. 17, '64
Garrett, J. 41, Aug. 19, '64
Garm, J. W, 101, Aug. 19, '64
Galliger, F. 101, Aug. 21, '64
Gamble, O. J, 77, Aug. 22, '64
Gallagher, E, 48, Aug. 22, '64
Gibson, J. O, 56, Aug. 29, '64
Graham, J, 56, Aug. 30, '64
Geary, D, 184, Aug. 30, '64
Glass, W, 55, Aug. 31, '64
Groves, J. F, 45, Aug. 31, '64
Griffith, A, 54, Sept. 1, '64
Granger, E. H, 55, Sept. 2, '64
Goslin, E. H. 4, Sept. 3, '64
Giles, C, 77, Sept. 4, '64
Gross, G. W, 79, Sept. 4, '64
Galbrath, C, 11, Sept. 26, '64
Garrison, W, 8, Sept 10, '64
Gallagher, W, 5, Sept. 11, '64
Griffin, J. C, 5, Sept. 14, '64
Grearhan, S, 142, Sep 17, '64
Griffin, D, 11, Sept. 18, '64
Gilbert, H, 53, Sept. 20, '64
Gooby, F. J, 7, Sep. 21, '64
Gooman, F, 55, Sep. 22, '64
Grubbs, J, 103, Sep. 25, '64
Gibson, J, 11, Sept. 26, '64
Glum, W, 101, Sept. 26, '64
Grear, K, 73, Sept. 26, '64
Gilbert, D, 138, Sep. 28, '64
Garret, F, 139, Sept. 29, '64
Gimpering, W, 79, Oct. 1, '64
Grant, M, 18, Oct. 7, '64
Griffin, J, 56, Oct. 10, '64
Gimberling, J, 184, Oct. 11, '64
Greathouse, F, 14, Oc. 17, '64
Grubb, M. P, 83, Oc. 20, '64
Gilbert, A. F, 14, Oc. 20, '64
Grant, J, 6, Oct. 26, '64
Gause, R, 22, Oct, 27, '64
Gordin, R, 65, Nov. 4, '64
Green, W. S, 12, Nov. 7, '64
Giahr, P, 73, Nov. 27, '64
George, F, 118, Dec. 6, '64
Garrety, T H, 73, Jan 2, '65
Gates, J, 11, Jan. 7, '65
Grimmel, J H, 26, Jan. 11, '65
Gravistol, F B, 89, Feb. 4, '65
Hanson, F E, 119, Ap. 7, '64
Herbert, O A, 73, Ap. 10, '64

Hoffneoster, L, 16, Apl. 14, '64
Hamilton, G J, L,4, Ap. 21, '64
Hall, I 8, Ap. 24, '64
Hessimer, P, 73, Ap. 27, '64
Hannius, J, 3, May, 10, '64
Heagen, J, 2, May 10, '64
Hanna, F, 4, June 15, '64
Hammer, P C, 18, June 17, '64
Harts, J, 51, June 19, '64
Hooks, F, 103, June 24, '64
Hilm, H, 50, June 25, '64
Hammer, J, 73, June 27, '64
Howard, J, 83, June 30, '64
Henderson, A, 58, July 1, '64
Hollebaugh, W, 57, July 1, '64
Hastings, J, 118, July 2, '64
Horner, D, 13, July 5, '64
Holly, E F, 57 July 8, '64
Harrington, J, 55, July 12, '64
Hight, S. C, 55, July 16, '64
Hughes, J, 118, July 17, '64
Hall, B, 105, July 17, '64
Herman, J, 13, July 18, '64
Hazlett, J, 4, July 18, '64
Hester, J. P, 7, July 18, '64
Heth, R, 2, July 20, '64
Harrington, W. J, 3, July 22, '64
Haller, P, 103, July 22, '46
Harry, P. D, 57, July 23, '64
Hollenbach, J. A, 55, July 23, '64,
Hall, H, 53, July 24, '64
Haller, H, 73, July 24, '64
Hartlick, C, 99, July 27, '64
Henfliger, V, 14, July 28, '64
Hobbs, A, 141, July 28, '64
Hill, P 101, July 28, '64
Hoover, J, 18, July 29, '64
Holland, J, 143 July 30, '64
Helb, J, 73, July 31, '64

Hardinger, W, 147, July 31 '64
Hill, T, 18, July 31, '64
Haus, J, 116, Aug, 1, '64
Helson. G. 2. Aug. 1, '64
Haflingle, J, 91, Aug. 5. '64
Hick, G, 12, Aug. 6, '64
Hahn, C, 14, Aug. 8, '64
Hull, H, 149, Aug. 8, '64
Hunter, L, 63, Aug. 8, '64
Harden, M, Home Guard, Aug. 9, '64
Huffman, C, 7, Aug. 11, '64
Hickey, D. C, 3, Aug. 11, '64
Hudson, J, 76, Aug. 11, '64
Harden, 184, Aug. 13, '64
Hoffmaster, G, 20, Aug. 14, '64
Heinback, S, 116, Aug. 15, '64
Hollinbeck, D, 101, Aug. 17, '64
Honigar, C, 55, Aug. 18, '64
Henry, R. W, 4, Aug. 20, '64
Hill, J. S, 2. Aug. 22, '64
Hollinsworth, J, 8, Aug. 22, '64
Hofmaster, L, 73, Aug. 23, '64
Hzeuflucy, J, 26, Aug. 23, '64
Hadurc, R, 119, Aug. 24, '64
Hagan, T, 103, Aug. 25, '64
Hurling, A, 57, Aug. 25, '64
Hammer, J, 3, Aug. 26, '64
Hoy, J, 101, Aug. 27, '64
Hozen, M, 101, Aug. 27, '64
Houseman, G, 118, Aug. 28, '64
Holliman, W, 102, Aug. 30, '64
Hopes, W, 9, Aug. 30, '64
Havert, B, 52 Aug. 31, '64
Hilliger, C, 63, Sept. 1, '64
Hill, E. 110, Sept. 1, '64
Henry, A. B, 103, Sept. 1, '64
Hobson, B. F, 7, Sept. 2, '64

Harmon, J, 14, Sept. 2, '64
Harris, A, 2, Sept. 2, '64
Honeikeer, J,119,Sept.2,'64
Hickenbrocht, J, 2, Sept. 3, '64
Hughes, J, 11, Sept. 3, '64
Hover, S. P, 7, Sept. 3, '64
Hunter, C, 3, Sept. 3, '64
Holmes, S, 140, Sept. 5, '64
Hutton, J, 118, Sept. 6, '64
Hazel, G, 2, Sept. 2, '64
Hecker, G, 6, Sept. 9, '64
Henry, O. H, 2, Sept. 11,'64
Hauedpat, J. H, 68, Sept. 12, '64
Hopkins, G. R, 50, Sept.12, '64
Hansey, G, 90, Sept. 18, '64
Hooker, W, 8, Sept. 18, '64
Holdhaus, C, 63, Sept.18,'64
Houghlough, J,143,Sept.21, '64
Hill, I, 11, Sept. 21, '64
Hankel, J, 6, Sept. 21, '64
Hartzel, F, 7, Sept. 21, '64
Howay, I, 145, Sept. 22, '64
Houston, D, 4, Sept. 22, '64
Harmony, J, 168,Sep.23,'64
Hemuschalt, W, 149, Sept. 27, '64
Hibbaus, J, 99, Sept. 27,'64
Haughey, J, 69, Sept.27,'64
Hamilton, B,183,Sep.29,'64
Holden, I, 7, Sept. 30, '64
Harper, R, 103, Sept, 30,'64
Haman, J, 118, Oct. 2, '64
Hicks, J. F, 14, Oct. 3, '64
Haynes, J, 184, Oct. 4, '64
Hammond, J, 10, Oct. 5,'64
Hill, S. M, 141, Oct. 5. '64
Heller, S, 64, Oct. 7, '64
Howe, M. A, 112, Oct. 7,'64
Hand, H, 55, Oct. 8, '64
Holdin, P, 12, Oct. 9, '64

Hayes, J, 15, Oct. 9, '64
Hands, J, 116, Oct. 10, '64
Hall, E, 77, Oct. 11, '64
Hennessey, P, 49,Oct.12,'64
Hunbacle, J, 116,Oct.12,'64
Hoburg, A. J, 2, Oct. 13,'64
Hannassoy, A,55,Oct.14,'64
Hall, A, 118, Oct. 14, '64
Hoover, S, 79, Oct. 15,'64
Hoffman, S, 64, Oct. 15,'64
Hoppy, G, 101, Oct. 16,'64
Harty, J, 148, Oct. 17, '64
Horton, S, 11, Oct. 18, '64
Hess, G, 118, Oct. 20, '64
Hepsey, M, 73, Oct. 20, '64
Hunter, J, 14, Oct 20, '64
Hunter, F, 5, Oct 24, '64
Hart, J, 7, Oct. 26, '64
Hartwich, J, 2, Oct. 26, '64
Hasflook, H. A,6,Oct.28,'64
Hachette, J, 50, Oct. 30,'64
Hoover, J, 90, Oct. 31, '64
Haggerty, W. R.7,Nov.4,'64
Hart, M, 11, Nov. 7, '64
Hyatt, J, 118, Dec. 3, '64
Healey, J. B,100,Dec.11,'64
Hammond,W,20,Dec 18,'64
Henman, E.L, 5,Feb.17,'65
Hummell, J, 87, Feb.24,'65
Hawks, N, 101,Sept. 15,'64
Hawks, A, 101,Sept. 27,'64
Ishart, N, 18. Mar. 23, '64
Ingersol, S, 3, May 1, '64
Irwin, F, 16, Oct. 8, '64
Ireton, S. R,138,Oct. 10,'64
Iobia, J, 55, Oct. 11, '64
Irvine, W, 184, Oct. 26, '64
Johnson, J. J, 45, Mar.29,'64
Johnson, C, 90, Ap. 10, '64
Johnson, J, 2, Ap. 15, '64
Jacobs, J, 2, May 9, '64
Jones, W, 26, June 11, '64
Jones, O, 4, June 17, '64
Johnson, W, 3, June 22, '64

WHO DIED AT ANDERSONVILLE. xiii

Jones, R, 103, June 28, '64
Johnison, A. G, 103, July 5, '64
Jordan, D. W, 103, July 5, '64
Johnson, D, 45, July 18, '64
Jennings, F, 45, July 18, '64
Jones, W, 55, July 24, '64
John, T, 54, July 27, '64
Jones, J, 79, July 27, '64
Johnson, J. W, 50, Aug. 2, '64
Johnson, —, 13, Aug. 2, '64
Jamison, W, 103, Aug. 3, '64
Jobins, R, 101, Aug. 5, '64
Johnson, H, 21, Aug. 11, '64
Jacobs, B. G, 150, Aug. 13, '64
Jobes, R, 100, Aug. 16, '64
Jones, T, 101, Aug. 19, '64
Jones, S, 49, Aug. 22, '64
Jaslin, J, 145, Aug. 25, '64
Jobes, J, 77, Aug. 25, '64
Jarmier, C, 7, Aug. 26, '64
Johnson, C, 53, Sept. 2, '64
Johnson, J, 45, Sept. 10, '64
Jolly, J, 101, Sept. 16, '64
Johnson, P, 63, Sept. 20, '64
Jordan, J. M, 149, Sept. 20, '64
Jeffries, C. 4, Sept. 29, '64
Jones, F, 101, Sept. 29, '64
Jones, A, 27, Oct. 16, '64
Johnson, W, 184, Oct 17, '64
Jordon, T, 148, Oct. 24, '64
Janks, C, 115, Oct. 26, '64
Jobson, L, 118, Nov. 14, '64
Jack, J. R. 7, Dec. 24, '64
Kelly, C. H, 71, Mar. 1, '64
Kelly, W. G, 13, Mar. 30, '64
Kuntzleman, G, 63, Mar. 31, '64
Kenny, Wm, 12, May 1, '64
Kylee, W, 5, June 10, '64
Kelly, P, 73, June 12, '64
Knight, J, 7, June 17, '64
Kelloe, M, 8, June 22, '64
Kenean, M A, 14, June 29, '64

King, C, 6, July 8, '64
Keich, H, 54, July 12, '64
Klink, A, 101, July, 13, '64
Kimp, E, 103, July 17, '64
Kuston, E, 103, July 20, '64
Kirer, H. H, 63, July 20, '64
Kagman, J. G, 45, July 28, '64
Kuffman, S. D, 45, July 30, '64
Kauf, J, 2, Aug. 2, '64
Kelly, E. F, Aug. 148, 6, '64
Kawell, E, 18, Aug. 9, '64
Keys, A, 16, Aug. 9, '64
Kester, L, 149, Aug. 10, '64
Kelly, G. 13, Aug. 12, '64
Kaher, R, 90, Aug. 12, '64
Keister, J. M, 103, Aug. 15, '64
Keeley, W, 13, Aug. 15, '64
Kauffman, B, 45, Aug. 18, '64
Kemper, J, 73, Aug. 18, '64
Kiger, W, 3, Aug. 22, '64
Kenler, A. N, 67, Aug. 22, '64
Kniver, G, 184, Aug. 22, '64
Kreigte, H, 11, Aug. 23, '64
Kock, J, 103, Aug 24, '64
Krader, W. O, 55, Aug. 27, '64
King, M, 3, Aug. 27, '64
Keller, A, 9, Aug. 31, '64
Keller, M, 105, Sept, 1, '64
Kyle, W, 118, Sept. 4, '64
Kinsman, G. P, 148, Sept. 8, '64
Kaufman, G, 45, Sept. 17, '64
Kennedy, J. P, 101, Sept. 17, '64
Kripp, W, 121, Sept. 18, '64
Kimmick, Z, 145, Sep 23, '64
Karney, L, 50, Sept. 24, '64
Kerr, B, 149, Oct. 4, '64
Kirby, G. A, 101, Oct. 4, '64
Kline, R, 184, Oct. 6, '64
Kenedy, G, 152, Oct. 8, '64
King, M, 11, Oct. 11, '64
Kirkwood, H, 101, Sept. 11, '64

Krisepur, C. 89, Sept. 14, '64
Kurtz, J, 55, Oct. 21. '64
King, R. P, 55, Oct. 23, '64
Kelly, E, 7, Oct. 24, '64
King, R, 6, Oct. 25, '64
Knot, J, 184, Feb. 23, '65
Koon, M, 2, July 28, '64
Kavinfard, J. C, 5, Sept, 14, '64
Lowler, S, 2, May 4, '64
Leiser, L, 13, Mar. 21, '64
Lancaster, E, 14, Mar. 30, '64
Luck, W, 11, April, 2, '64
Lynch, A. 6, April, 14, '64
Lenard, M. 13, April 26, '64
Lord, G, M, 141, April 27, '64
Lachey. J. 183, June 20, '64
Leach, J, 3, June, 23, '64
Lasimer, J, 11, July 9, '64
Link, P, 98, July 14, '64
Long, A. 118, July 14, '64
Lewis, E, 101, July 16. '64
Leonard, G, 49, July 17. '64
Logand. B, 90, July 17, '64
Lee, J, 13, July 18, '64
Ladbeater, J. 7. July 21. '64
Leisk, K, 144. July 24, '64
Large, D. B. E, 101, July 30, '64
Lambert, W, 4, July 31, '64
Larrison, W, 14, Aug. 4, '64
Lewis, A, 3, Aug. 5, '64
Laughlin, J, 101, Aug. 6, '64
Lachman, C. 73, Aug. 6, '64
Livingston, J. R, 2, Aug. 6, '64
Long, A, 55, Aug. 10, '64
Loudin. H. W, 14, Aug. 10, '64
Leavk, H, 116, Aug. 11, '64
Ledwick, T. M, 139, Aug. 15, '64
Logan, W, 97, Aug. 17, '64
Louder, S, 101, Aug. 18, '64
Laylon, S, 184, Aug. 18, '64

Lamb, C, 91, Aug. 19, '64
Lane, A, 6, Aug. 18, '64
Labrinth. G, 2, Aug. 19, '64
Laders, H, 90. Aug. 20, '64
Leach, J, 49, Aug. 23, '64
Light, S, 143, Aug. 25, '64
Latchan, D, 4, Aug. 28, '64
La Bolt, J, 21, Aug. 29, '64
Lochery, A, 14, Aug. 30, '64
Lemon, J, 76, Sept. 5, '64
Lockard, J, 45, Sept. 5, '64
Leply, C, 103, Sept. 11, '64
Laman, F, 49, Sept. 14, '64
Laughman, J. S, 1, Sept. 15, '64
Lippish, J, 174, Sept 16, '64
Logue, S, 26, Sept. 18, '64
Leary, C, 83, Sept. 19, '64
Loler, J, 4, Sept. 24, '64
Layton, P, 110, Sept. 30, '64
Lutz, P, 21, Sept. 30, '64
Luboss, C, 116, Sept. 30, '64
Lemon, W, 140, Oct. 3, '64
Long, W, 67, Oct. 4, '64
Lancaster, C, 119, Oct. 9, '64
Lynch, N. J, 3. Oct. 9, '64
Labur, R, 7, Oct. 10, '64
Luchford, R, 143, Oct. 11, '64
Lang, J, 110, Oct. 13. '64
Lenchlin, J, 5, Oct. 16, '64
Lantz, W, 7, Oct. 21, '64
Lewis, J, 14, Oct. 26, '64
Luther, J, 4, Nov. 1, '64
Lego, G, 12, Nov. 6, '64
Ladd, A, 53, Nov. 7, '64
Lape, J, 18, Nov. 28, '64
Lewis, D. S, 53, Dec. 2, '64
Lindsay, D, 77, Jan. 9, '65
Lafferty, W, Art. June 9, '64
Maynard. J, 105, Mar. 27, '64
Missile, V, 47, Mar. 28, '64
Miller, D, 13, Mar. 29, '64
Martin, J. H, 14, Ap. 4, '64
McEntrye, W, 51, Ap. 10, '64

WHO DIED AT ANDERSONVILLE. XV

Marple, S. I., 14, Ap. 17, '64
McKissich, J, 23, Ap. 18, '64
Myers, G, 1, Ap. 22, '64
McKeever, L. E, 71, Ap. 25, '64
McDonald, R, 23, Ap. 28, '64
McCarty, J, 18, Ap. 28, '64
McQueeny, W, 79, May 9, '64
Moyer, J, 2, May 10, '64
McKenee, D, 63, May 11, '64
McHose, J, 4, June 12, '64
Miller, H, 8, June 13, '64
Mullholland, J, 101, June 15, '64
Moorooi, W. H, 3, June 16, '64
Matchett, J. J, 101, June 16, '64
Marrow, J, 101, June 19, '64
McCutcheon, J, 4, June 20, '64
Melton, W, 19, June 20, '64
Myers, F, 27, June 22, '64
Myers, P, 76, June 23, '64
Morton, S, 79, June 24, '64
McCate, J, 3, June 24, '64
McKay, M. J, 103, Jun 24, '64
Murray, J, 67, June 26, '64
Martin, A. J, 4, June 26, '64
Morris, J, 18, June 26, '64
McManes, J, 77, June 29, '64
Mipes, J, 101, June 30, '64
Morris, G, 77, June 30, '64
Marsh, D, 50, July 2, '64
McCane, C, 14, July 3, '64
McRath, J, 48, July 8, '64
Morris, C, 53, July 9, '64
McClaskey, J. E, 4, July 10, '64
Malteson, B, 57, July 11, '64
Madden, D, 149, July 11, '64
Myers, M, 103, July 13, '64
Meaher, E. H, 155, July 17, '64
McKon, J, 101, July 17, '64
Mihows, J, 138, July 17, '64
Mawny, J, 1, July 20, '64
McCarron, J, 4, July 21, '64
Myers, J, 116, July 22, '64
Major, W, 103, July 22, '64
Martin, G, 45, July 25, '64
McDermott, J, 70, July 26, '64
Magee, J, 103, July 28, '64
Moore, M. G, 1, July 29, '64
Margut, M, 6, July 30, '64
McKever, J, 100, July 31, '64
McFarland, J, 112, July 31, '64
Moan, J, 101, Aug. 2, '64
McKeomer, S, 73, Aug. 2, '64
McKiral, J, 14, Aug. 3, '64
Mathews, C. W, 145, Aug. 4, '64
Moore, M, 71, Aug. 4, '64
McDevitt, J, 3, Aug. 5, '64
Miller, H, 14, Aug. 5, '64
Mills, W, 150, Aug. 6, '64
Muldaney, M, 96, Aug. 6, '64
Martin, J, 103, Aug. 8, '64
Measles, J, 103, Aug. 8, '64
Mardis, J. L, 11, Aug. 9, '64
McCaffrey, J. H, 3, Aug. 9, '64
Martin, C, 8, Aug. 9, '64
Money, H. F, 103, Aug. 10, '64
Mohr, J. R, 103, Aug. 11, '64
McCarty, D, 101, Aug. 12, '64
McGee, J, 14, Aug. 12, '64
McCough, L. C, 18, Aug. 14, '64
Miller, J, 101, Aug. 15, '64
McCann, J, 3, Aug. 15, '64
Miller, S, 2, Aug. 15, '64
Montgomery, R, 62, Aug. 16, '64
McCullen, S, 4, Aug. 16, '64

Mulchey, J. A, 50, Aug, 17, '64
Mann, J, 119, Aug. 17, '64
McPherson, D, 103, Aug. 17, '64
Moore, C, 103, Aug. 18, '64
McCrackin, J, 53, Aug. 19, '64
McLaughlin, J, 4, Aug. 20, '64
McWilliams, H, 82, Aug. 22, '64
Martin, J, 103, Aug. 22, '64
McGarr, J, 118, Aug. 22, '64
McKee, M, 141, Aug. 24, '64
Mannie, M, 73, Aug. 24, '64
McKeon, J, 77, Aug. 24, '64
McGlane, H, 143, Aug. 26, '64
McGuigan, H. C, 7, Aug. 26, '64
Marks, P, 143, Aug. 27, '64
Moore, M. J, 107, Aug. 28, '64
Moyer, W. M, 55, Aug. 28, '64
Miller, J. L, 53, Aug. 28, '64
McAfee, J, 72, Aug. 28, '64
Moore, T, 69, Aug. 29, '64
Martin, J, 77, Aug. 30, '64
Musser, J, 77, Aug. 30, '64
Moser, S, 103, Aug. 30, '64
Morris, J, 183, Aug. 30, '64
Maxton, W, 50, Aug. 31, '64
Millinger, J. H, 7, Sep. 1, '64
Moorhead, J. S, 104, Sept. 2, '64
Myers, H, 9. Sept. 3, '64
Moran, L, 3, Sept. 3, '64
Moyer, W, 8, Sept. 5, '64
Mays, A. J, 118, Sept. 5, '64
Murphy, A, 13, Sept. 6, '64
McKnight, J, 18, Sept. 6, '64
Miller, J, 101, Sept. 8, '64
Mullings, U, 145, Sept. 8, '64
Munayer, W, 13, Sept. 8, '64

Mehaffy, J. M, 16, Sept. 8, '64
McCarty, W, 2, Sept. 8, '64
McLane, T, 12, Sept. 8, '64
McKirk, J. C, 119, Sep. 8, '64
Mansfield, J, 101, Sept. 8, '64
Myers, A, 118, Sept. 10, '64
Magill, H. J, 103, Sept. 11, '64
Morrison, J, 146, Sept. 12, '64
McKinney, D, 90, Sept. 13, '64
Moritye, A, 118, Sept. 14, '64
McCullough, T. M, 101, Sept. 15, '64
Maynard, A, 3, Sept. 17, '64
McCall, W, 22, Sept. 18, '64
McCullough, S, 138, Sept. 19, '64
Mayhorn, F, 20, Sept. 19, '64
Marsh, W, 149, Sept. 20, '64
Myers, J, 138, Sept. 20, '64
McQuigley, J, 101, Sept. 22, '64
Mead, H. G, 184, Sept. 23, '64
Martin, J, 17, Sept. 23, '64
Morris, J, 54, Sept. 23, '64
Morgan, J. C, 2, Sept. 24, '64
McCool, B, 118, Sept. 24, '64
Morgan, J. C, 2, Sept. 24, '64
Murry, W. M, 1, Sept. 25, '64
Mason, J, 112, Sept. 27, '64
Myers, D. G, 37, Sept. 27, '64
Mussin, J, 90, Sept. 30, '64
Morgan, C, 45, Sept. 30, '64
McClarry, J, 101, Oct. 1, '64
McElroy, W, 13, Oct. 1, '64
Mase, J, 48, Oct. 4, '64
McGraw, J, 3, Oct. 6, '64
Miller, H. F, 79, Oct. 6, '64
Miller, W, 18, Oct. 7, '64
McKinney, J. W, 118, Oct. 7, '64
McCleaf, W, 7, Oct. 10, '64
Marker, W, H, 118, Oct. 10, '64

Martin, J, 7, Oct. 11, '64
Mullen, J, 7, Oct. 11, '64
Mattis, A, 133, Oct. 12, '64
Moore, C. H, 13, Oct. 13, '64
Morton, G. H, 108, Oct. 16, '64
Maxwell, S, 14, Oct. 15, '64
Masses, W, 16, Oct. 16, '64
McKnight, J, 118, Oct. 16, '64
Mitchell, J. S, 55, Oct. 17, '64
Mansfield, G, 101, Oct. 18, '64
McClay, J, 11, Oct. 20, '64
McBride, J, 2, Oct. 22, '64
Marshall, L, 184, Oct. 23, 64
Moore, S, 101, Oct. 24, '64
Moore, J, 13, Oct. 15, '64
McWeese, J. H, 100, Oct. 26, '64
Miller, F, 54, Oct. 26, '64
Midy, J, 20, Oct. 30, '64
Morrow, J. G, 107, Oct. 31, '64
McCann, J, 11, Oct. 31, '64
Moore, W, 164, Oct. 31, '64
Mulligan, J, 7, Oct. 31, '64
McCune, J, 67, Nov. 8, '64
McClush, J, 97, Nov. 8, '64
Manse, M, 53, Nov. 13, '64
McCray, J, 145, Nov. 14, '64
Mahan, D, 118, Nov. 18, '64
Matt, H, 12, Nov. 19, '64
Mullen, W, 166, Nov. 20, '64
Murray, W, 14, Dec. 8, '64
McIntyre, J, 55, Dec. 24, '64
Myers, B. D, 52, Dec. 26, '64
Mathews, J, 6, Jan. 29, '65
Maloy, J. M, 184, Feb. 5, '65
McGurger, J, 20, Feb. 9, '65
Myers, H, 87, Feb. 23, '65
McDowell, N, 9, Feb. 13, '65
McGarrah, R, 103, Feb. 21, '65
Morton, B, 7, Aug. 3, '64
Myers, J, 148, Sept. 16, '64
Morton, J. B, Art. Mar. 20, '64
Nine, J, 54, Ap. 14, '64

Nolt, W, 6, July 4, 64
Nurich, W, 3, July 16, '64
Newell, G. S, 183, July 20, '64
Nicholson, W, 1, July 29, '64
Naylor, G. W, 13, Aug. 7, '64
Nickleson, B, 16, Aug. 14, '64
Neal, H. P, 90, Aug. 17, '64
Nichle, C, 37, Aug. 17, '64
Naylor, S, 20, Sept. 8, '64
Noble, J, 184, Sept. 16, '64
Neff, J, 4, Sept. 21, '64
Nelson, G, 55, Oct. 1, '64
Nelson, J, 145, Oct. 4, '64
Newbery, J, 20, Oct. 11, '64
Neighbor, J, 7, Oct. 14, '64
Nelson, A, 160, Oct. 17, '64
Noble, T, 19, Oct. 21, '64
Neuk, W, 12, Oct. 30, '64
Nichols, G, 20, Nov. 3, '64
Nealy, J, 143, Feb. 10, '64
Nolord, D, 54, Oct. 14, '64
Oyley, R, 15, Mar. 30, '64
Osborne, S. R, 4, Ap. 7, '64
Oglesby, J, 4, Ap. 19, '64
Ort, M, 21, June 11, '64
O'Neal, J, 69, June 13, '64
Oswald, S, 55, June 28, '64
O'Connor, —83, July 11, '64
O'Neal, J, 63, July 12, '64
Olnun, H, 2, July 21, '64
O'Conor, H, 49, July 24, '64
Owens, G. H, 7, July 28, '64
Offleback, Z, 90, Aug. 9, '64
Oliver, W, 103, Aug. 9, '64
O'Harra, M, 101, Aug. 17, '64
O'Connel, W, 1, Aug. 20, '64
O'Harra, I, 150, Aug. 22, '64
Oiler, S, 103, Aug. 24, '64
O'Rourk, C, 109, Aug. 29, '64
Otto, J, 5, Aug. 28, '64
Osborne, J. M, 101, Sept. 2, '64
Otto, H, 184, Sept. 18, '64
Orwin, N. V. B, 149, Sept. 29, '64

Owens, E, 50, Sept. 20, '64
Osborne, E, —, Oct. 12, '64
Ocuranat,—, 184, Nov. 6, '64
Peak, A, 57, Mar. 9, '64
Patterson, R, 2, Mar. 18, '64
Parker, J. M, 76, Mar. 23, '64
Petrishey, H, 54, Ap. 12, '64
Pry, L, 4, Ap. 28, '64
Powell, F, 18, June 12, '64
Page, J, 183, June 27, '64
Porter, D, 101, June 28, '64
Persons, J. T, 103, July 5, '64
Painter, J. G, 26, July 11, '64
Painter, S, 63, July, 17, '64
Patterson, R, 101, July 27, '64
Picket, J. J. C, 3, July 28, '64
Pratt, F, 14, July 28, '64
Plymier, W, 20, July 28, '64
Page, J, 112, July 31, '64
Powell, H, 102, Aug. 1, '64
Prosser, J, 63, Aug. 11, '64
Philips, J. B, 101, Aug. 14, '64
Pence, G, 103, Aug. 17, '64
Parish, J. A, 184, Aug. 17, '64
Porter, S, 4, Aug. 20, '64
Pream, H, 149, Aug. 22, '64
Palmer, W, 140, Aug. 22, '64
Poole, G, 52, Aug. 22, '64
Piper, M, 13, Aug. 22, '64
Phillips, J. N, 1, Aug. 23, '64
Peterson, G, 103, Aug. 25, '64
Peur, J, 5, Aug. 25, '64
Parker, W. A, 102, Aug. 25, '64
Patton, H. W, 2, Aug. 26, '64
Potts, E, 183, Aug. 28, '64
Perkins, N, 103, Aug. 29, '64
Powell, A. F, 149, Sept. 6, '64
Pricht, F, 87, Sept. 8, '64
Peek, C. W, 145, Sept. 14,
Perril, F, 101, Sept. 16, '64
Palmer, A, 143, Sept. 19, '64
Perego, W, Sept. 24, '64

Phipps, J. A, 57, Sept. 25, '64
Price, G. 106, Sept. 30, '64
Penstoch, A, 144, Oct. 9, '64
Powell, J, 101, Oct. 18, '64
Price, O, 109, Oct. 20, '64
Phay, M, 69, Oct. 21, '64
Porterfield, J. K, 5, Oct. 23, '64
Phillips, F, 61, Oct. 29, '64
Prince, L, 183, Oct. 30, '64
Pees, M. F, 145, Nov. 2, '64
Penn, W. B, 18, Nov. 6, '64
Phelps, W, 4, Nov. 8, '64
Permier, W, 118, Nov. 18, '64
Pryor, W, 11, Nov. 28, '64
Palman, H, 1, Dec. 30, '64
Perry, H, 121, Jan. 2, '65
Prichett, J, 72. Jan. 3, '65
Potter, B. F, 148, Jan. 18, '65
Quinby, L. C, 76, Aug. 24, '64
Reed, S, 4, Mar. 15, '64
Robertson, J, 119, Mar. 23, '64
Rosenburg, H, 49, Mar. 24, '64
Reiger, J, 83, Mar. 26, '64
Richpeder, A, 13, Ap. 2, '64
Ray, W, 8, Ap. 18, '64
Rineheart, J, 18, May 5,
Russell, F, 4, May 5, '64
Rinebolt, J, 18, May 5. '64
Robinson, C. W, 150, May 7, '64
Ramsey, J. D, 103, June 11, '64
Rush, S, 18, June 14, '64
Robinson, W, 77, June 14, '64
Ray, A, 77, June 17, '64
Roush, P, 101, June 20, '64
Repert, F, 2, June 26, '64
Roat, J, 54, June 28, '64
Rhodes, F, 79, July 1, '64
Revek, J. E, 5, July 5, '64
Ragart J, 13, July 7, '64

Rugh, M. J, 103, July 8, '64
Robbins, R, 69, July 13, '64
Reiner, L, 5, July 23, '64
Ringwalt, F. J, 79, July 27, '64
Ragan, C, 73, July 30, '64
Ray, J. R, 184, Aug. 1, '64
Reese, S, 103, Aug. 1, '64
Riche, J, 103, Aug. 6, '64
Ruthfan, J, 2, Aug. 7, '64
Rice, S, 101, Aug. 11, '64
Ross, D, 103, Aug. 12, '64
Robinson, J, 99, Aug. 12, '64
Rose, B, 13, Aug. 12, '64
Ryers, I, 72, Aug. 14, '64
Robins, J, 2, Aug. 15, '64
Reider, F, 7, Aug. 16, '64
Richards, E, 143, Aug. 16, '64
Rease, J, 103, Aug. 17, '64
Richards, J, 1, Aug. 17, '64
Rodgers, F, 20, Aug. 20, '64
Robbins, G, 106, Aug. 21, '64
Rager, J. L, 110, Aug. 22, '64
Reynolds, J, 14, Aug. 22, '64
Rowe, E, 103, Aug. 24, '64
Richards, G, 13, Aug. 25, '64
Runnells, J, 6, Aug. 25, '64
Reem, A, 188, Aug. 25, '64
Reese, D, 148, Aug. 25, '64
Raeff, F, 1, Aug. 26, '64
Richardson, 61, Aug. 26, '64
Reese, O, 143, Aug. 28, '64
Rueff, J, 103, Aug. 29, '64
Redmire, H, 98, Aug. 30, '64
Robins, G, 62, Aug. 30, '64
Richardson, H, 103, Aug. 31, '64
Richards, D, 18, Sept. 1, '64
Rice, E, 7, Sept. 3, '64
Roads, F, 101, Sept. 3, '64
Rathborn, K, 2, Sept. 6, '64
Rowlings, 20, Sept. 8, '64
Russell, S. A, 79, Sept. 12, '64
Ray, A, 149, Sept. 12, '64

Richards, J, 106, Sept. 12, '64
Root, D, 48, Sept. 14, '64
Reader, C, 51, Sept. 16, '64
Rex, G, 18, Sept. 17, '64
Richie, H, 11, Sept. 23, '64
Renamer, N. H, 87, Sept. 23, '64
Richards, J, 113, Sept. 23, '64
Reed, R, 103, Sept. 24, '64
Ramsey, B, 84, Sept. 25, '64
Richards, Z, 53, Sept. 25, '64
Reid, Z, 55, Oct. 1, '64
Rudy, E. F, 87, Oct. 10, '64
Ramsey, W, 87, Oct. 13, '64
Roundabush, H. B, 55, Oct. 14, '64
Rochkerrell, A, 2, Oct. 15, '64
Ruff, B, 72, Oct. 17, '64
Runkle, J. A, 20, Oct. 18, '64
Rudy, J, 13, Oct. 18, '64
Rolson, Z, 118, Oct. 22, '64
Riffle, S. G, 189, Oct. 25, '64
Richardson, A, 144, Oct. 27, '64
Rowland, M, 111, Nov. 6, '64
Rapp, A, 45, Nov. 15, '64
Ruth, B. I, 23, Nov. 16, '64
Rothe, C, 101, Dec. 1, '64
Reese, D, 7, Dec. 29, '64
Reed, W. S, 118, Jan. 1, '65
Smith, M. D, 18, Ap. 5, '64
Smith, G, 5, Ap. 28, '64
Smith, W, 4, May 4, '64
Smith, F, 19, May 4, '64
Stifflen, W. J, 12, May 6, '64
Screna, H, 4, May 10, '64
Smith, D, 11, June 14, '64
Slough, H, 53, June 16, '64
Stevens, A, 13, ——
Sherwood, C. H, 4, June 17, '64
Stall, S, 78, June 17, '64
Say, R, 4, June 17, '64
Stell, J. S, 7, June 19, '64

Scoles, Neil, 27, June 20, '64
Sims, B, 14, June 22, '64
Shoap, J, 2, June 24, '64
Springer, J, 101, June 28, '64
Stewart, J. B, 103, June 29, '64
Scott, A, 150, July 1, '64
Schingerz, J, 73, July 1, '64
Skinner, J. A, 13, July 2, '64
Stamp, A, 11, July 4, '64
Smith, J, 51, July 6, '64
Shaw, W, 140, July 7, '64
Smalley, J, 112, July 7, '64
Secton, R. M, 103, July 9, '64
Sweet, H, 57, July 10, '64
Shoemaker, M, 148, July 10, '64
Sellers, W, 77, July 11, '64
Stone, W, 53, July 12, '64
Sannigaw, M, 13, July 15, '64
Smetser, J, 103, July 17, '64
Smalley, L, 58, July 19, '64
Stevens, —, 150, July 19, '64
Sicles, D, 116, July, 19, '64
Suders, J. S, 142, July 20, '64
Stopper, W, 16, July 20, '64
Stitenberger, F, 172, July 22, '64
Strance, D, 11, July 22, '64
Smith, J, 79, July 24, '64
Smith, O. C, 77, July 24, '64
Sullivan, T, 77, July 25, '64
Smith, F, 64, July 26, '64
Shafer, J. M, 84, July 26, '64
Shapley, G, 103, July 26, '64
Stickley, C, 53, July 27, '64
Shrively, E. S, 19, July 27, '64
Sheppard, E, 145, July 28, '64
Smith, S. M, 101, July 28, '64
Shaffer, P, 52, July 29, '64
Shister, F, 3, July 29, '64
Stein, J, 7, July 29, '64

Stran, J, 11, July 29, '64
Showe, R, 4, July, 30, '64
Stubbs, W. W, 101, July 30, '64
Scott, A, 22, July 31, '64
Schandler, J, 67, July 31, '64
Smith, P, 72, July 31, '64
Sale, T, 15, Aug. 2, '64
Shink, J, 81, Aug. 5, '64
Sullivan, E, 64, Aug. 5, '64
Sear, C, 14, Aug. 5, '64
Shomber, J, 11, Aug. 6, '64
Sheil, P, 61, Aug. 7, '64
Swarts, P, 27, Aug. 7, '64
Stiner, J, 22, Aug. 9, '64
Striker, F, 14, Aug. 9, '64
Swooerland, W, 184, Aug. 10, '64
Speek, A, 118, Aug. 10, '64
Shaffer, D, 13, Aug. 12, '64
Schrungost, A, 103, Aug. 12, '64
Shears, J. S, 149, Aug. 12, '64
Stibbs, W, 56, Aug. 12, '64
Sheepe, F, 18, Aug. 13, '64
Somerfield, N, 69, Aug. 14, '64
Steinbrook, A, 150, Aug. 15, '64
Spears, W. M, 2, Aug. 15, '64
Sheppard, N, 79, Aug. 16, '64
Shultz, F, 13, Aug. 17, '64
Shoop, G, 103, Aug. 19, '64
Smith, H. 26, Aug. 20, '64
Smith, W, 18, Aug. 20, '64
Swayer, M, 101, Aug. 22, '64
Spain, T, 118, Aug. 22, '64
Stover, J, 49, Aug. 22, '64
Stahler, B, 149, Aug. 22, '64
Snyder, J, 118, Aug. 22, '64
Sloate, E, 50, Aug. 23, '64
Shurley, H, 105, Aug. 23, '64
Sherwood, P, 84, Aug. 24, '64

Shelleto, R, 150, Aug. 25, '64
Shain, R, 118, Aug. 25, '64
Sturges, W. D, 79, Aug. 25, '64
Stahler, D, 4, Aug. 26, '64
Strichler, J. W, 11, Aug. 27 '64
Smith, J, 55, Aug. 28, '64
Sloughn, J. M, 15, Aug. 28, '64
Springer, J. S, 103, Aug. 29, '64
Shriver, B, 18, Aug. 30, '64
Singer, J, 2, Aug. 30, '64
Scoteton, J, 53, Aug. 31, '64
Sweeney, D, 14, Aug. 31, '64
Scott, W. B, 4, Aug. 31, '64
Streetman, J, 7, Sept. 2, '64
Steele, J, 62, Sept. 2, '64
Spencer, G, 23, Sept. 2, '64
Snyder, M. S, 183, Sept. 3, '64
Schwartze, G, 5, Sept. 3, '64
Stackhouse, D, 18, Sept. 4, '64
Sellers, H, 149, Sept. 5, '64
Shultz, J, 4, Sept. 5, '64
Smith, A. C, 7, Sept. 6, '64
Sassh, S, 81, Sept. 6, '64
Simpson, F, 53, Sept. 6, '64
Stumps, E, 105, Sept. 7, '64
Slade, E, 150, Sept. 7, '64
Shirk, M. B, 142, Sept. 11, '64
Simmons, W. H, 76, Sept. 12, '64
Spruel, E, 90, Sept. 13, '64
Smith, W, 2, Sept. 14, '64
Stella, J. F, 1, Sept. 15, '64
Steadman, N, 54, Sept. 17, '64
Shnably, J, 54, Sept. 18, '64
Shoup, S, 16, Sept. 18, '64
Sigwall, C, 79, Sept. 19, '64
Smith, C, 7, Sept. 20, '64
Stebins, Z, 7, Sept. 20, '64
Scott, D, 149, Sept. 21, '64
Snyder, A, 148, Sept. 23, '64
Steinholt, W, 38, Sept. 23, '64
Supple, C, M, 63, Sept. 25, '64
Surpluss, W, 13, Sept. 26, '64
Schick, C, 145, Sept. 27, '64
Sweeney, W. B, 13, Sept. 27, '64
Sanford, C, 69, Sept. 28, '64
Shepard, C, 118, Sept. 29, '64
Sloan, P, 115, Sept. 30, '64
Smith, J. S, 22, Oct. 1, '64
Strong, H, 55, Oct. 4, '64
Smith, E, 10, Oct. 4, '64
Snyder, W, 54, Oct. 8, '64
Stone, T, 121, Oct. 8, '64
Smallwood, C, 7, Oct. 8, '64
Small, H, 101, Oct. 10, '64
Smallman, J. W, 63, Oct. 11, '64
Steele, F. F, 20, Oct. 12, '64
Shank, A, 184, Oct. 13, '64
Smith, A, 22, Oct. 17, '64
Stephens, C. P, 11, Oct. 17, '64
Smith, H. W, 53, Oct. 20, '64
Smith, J, 57, Oct. 21, '64
Silvey, D, 18, Oct. 23, '64
Slyoff, H, 81, Oct. 23, '64
Sunderland, E, 1, Oct 26, '64
Stevenson, J, 111, Oct. 26, '64
Speck, O, 67, Oct. 30, '64
Smith, H, 183, Nov. 1, '64
Snodgrass, R. P, 145, Nov. 4, '64
Sallentine, M, 145, Nov. 4, '64
Syltyer, D, 20, Nov. 5, '64
Smith, W, 14, Nov. 6, '64
Shure, J. P, 184, Nov. 7, '64
Snively, J. W, 20, Nov. 7, '64
Scooell, J. H, 79, Nov. 8, '64
Sheffer, W, 118, Nov. 8, '64
Shitzer, G, 2, Nov. 17, '64
Sturkey, D, 184, Nov. 18, '64
Smith, J. F, 118, Dec. 3, '64

Skinner, S. O, 77, Dec. 4, '64
Shafar, S, 184, Dec. 13, '64
Stafford, W. W, 67, Dec. 19, '64
Sourbeer, J. E, 20, Jan. 3, '65
Sipe, F, 87, Feb. 5, '65
Stansfer, J, 1, Feb. 6, '65
Stanes, G. M, 20, Feb. 13, '65
Smith, G. M, 143, Feb. 14, '65
Slough, E. B, 1, Feb. 17, '65
Scott, N. B, 14, Feb. 17, '65
Sheridan, M, 103, Feb. 19, '65
Thistlewood, J, 73, Ap. 28, '64
Thompson, H, 57, June 10, '64
Thompson, A, 4, June 19, '64
Townsend, D, 18, June 22, '64
Tagontus, F, 90, June 28, '64
Tiser, L, 145, June 29, '64
Thompson, M, 103, July 7, '64
Titus, W, 171, July 14, '64
Todd, W, 103, July 17, '64
Thompson, J. S, 183, July 19, '64
Thompson, F, 18, July 22, '64
Trumbull, H, 3, July 25, '64
Thompson, J, 18, July 28, '64
Tinsdale, -, 149, July 28, '64
Tonson, J, 3, Aug. 4, '64
Thompson, W. W, 101, Aug. 9, '64
Thomas, F, 7, Aug. 11, '64
Thompson, J. B, 100, Aug. 17, '64
Thompson, F. A. B, 69, Aug. 19, '64
Telthousen, A. A, 148, Aug. 19, '64

Tautlinger, F, 53, Aug. 19, '64
Tubbs, E, 143, Aug. 22, '64
Teal, W, 11, Aug. 22, '64
Turner, J, 118, Aug. 25, '64
Thomas, E, 23, Aug. 30, '64
Thorp, L, 61, Aug. 31, '64
Tetter, H. M, 13, Sept. 6, '64
Tilt, N, 115, Sept. 12, '64
Teeter, C, 184, Sept. 13, '64
Tits, P, Sept. 17, '64
Thorp, D, 18, Sept. 19, '64
Thompson, H, 18, Sept. 20, '64
Tonson, E. P, 99, Sept. 25, '64
Thuck, F, 7, Sept. 29, '64
Tones, E, 145, Sept. 26, '64
Thompson, J, 90, Sept. 29, '64
Tibbitt, G, 69, Oct. 11, '64
Thatcher, R, 14, Oct. 16, '64
Thompson, J, 12, Oct. 24, '64
Trespan, P, 57, Nov. 2, '64
Townsend, C, 183, Oct. 18, '64
Taylor, C. N, 84, May 24, '64
Thompson, J. A. B, 69, Aug. 19, '64
Ubrick, J, 17, May 9, '64
Unknown, 77, Aug. 16, '64
Utter, W, 45, Nov. 23, '64
Vernon, S, 7, June 25, '64
Vogle, V, 78, July 24, '64
Vanholt, F, 13, July 29, '64
Vanderpool, F, 57, Aug. 26, '64
Van Campment, G, 52, Sept. 4, '64
Vail, G. B, 77, Sept. 9, '64
Vaugnan, J, 108, Sept. 15, '64
Varndale, J, 121, Sept. 16, '64
Vandeer, W. H, Sept. 24, '64
Van Duke, D. S, 103, Oct. 1, '64
Vanwikes, D, 6, Nov. 2, '64

Wilkins, A, 12, Mar. 17, '64
Williams, J, 83, June 28, '64
Waterman, J, 88, Mar. 23, '64
Wise, I, 18, Mar. 27, '64
Wheeler, J, 150, Apr. 11, '64
Warner, J, 76, Apr. 12, 64
Weed, A. B, 4, Ap. 17, '64
Wentworth, J, 83, Ap. 21, '64
Watson, F. F, 2, Ap. 22, '64
Wahl, J, 73, Ap. 23, '64
Wilson, J, 14, Ap. 27, '64
Williams, S, 18, May 3, '64
Wolf, J. H, 13, May 7, '64
Wright, J, 12, May 11, '64
Woodward, G. W, 3, June 13, '64
Wyant, H, 103, June 15, '64
Walters, C, 73, June 22, '64
Wike, A, 96, June 30, '64
Whitaker, W, 8, July 2, 64
Winsinger, S, 96, July 6, '64
Welder, L, 50, July 8, '64
Wallace, A, 116, July 10, '64
Wright, W. A, 20, July 14, '64
Woodruff, W. D, 103, July 16, '64
Wait, G, 1, July 16, '64
Walker, E, 7, July 19, '64
White, E. D, 5, July 21, '64
Wilson, A, 103, July 23, '64
White, M, 7, July 24, 64
Wilson, W, 43, July 24, '64
Winegarden, A, 73, July 27, '64
Wolf, A, 146, July 27, '64
Wisel, M, 18, July 28, '64
Wrudragagh, W, 4, July 28, '64
Ward, D, 138, July 30, '64
Williams, G, 54, July 31, '64
Willoughby, E, 148, Aug. 4, '64
Ward, P, 103, Aug. 5, '64
Wetherholt, C, 54, Aug. 7, '64

Waserum, G, 4, Aug. 7, '64
White, S, 14, Aug. 7, '64
Weaver, J, 90, Aug. 9, '64
Wilkes, S, 77, Aug. 11, '64
Wilson, W, 7, Aug. 12, '64
Weeks, D, 53, Aug. 14, '64
Williams, J, 7, Aug. 18, '64
Waterhouse, H, 3, Aug. 18, '64
Workman, A, 118, Aug. 19, '64
Whipple, H, 18, Aug. 20, '64
Wart, C, 143, Aug. 22, '64
Wineman, J, 17, Aug. 22, '64
Wible, P, 57, Aug. 23, '64
Walker, S. A, 103, Aug. 23, '64
Wick, R. C, 103, Aug. 25, '64
Woolslair, W. H, 77, Aug. 27, '64
White, J, 149, Aug. 27, '64
Woodford, J. A, 101, Aug. 27, '64
White, E, 103, Aug. 30, '64
Webb, J. S, 69, Aug. 31, '64
Walton, A, 4, Aug. 31, '64
Wallunk, S, 118, Sept. 3, '64
Warner, L, 5, Sept. 3, '64
Whitehead, J, 119, Sept. 4, '64
Wynn, H, 101, Sept. 4, '64
Wiggins, D, 2, Sept. 5, '64
Weekland, F, 101, Sept. 5, '64
Wade, G. N, 118, Sept. 5, '64
Weber, W, 116, Sept. 7, '64
White, D, 2, Sept. 10, '64
Wheeler, J, 7, Sept. 16, '64
Wheeler, C. C, Sept. 18, '64
Williams, W, 20, Sept. 20, '64
Wilson, (or Welson), W. H, 72, Sept. 21, '64
Warner, C. W, 184, Sept. 21, '64
Woolman, H, 18, Sept. 22, '64
Weston, J, 4, Sept. 23, '64

Wingate, C, 111, Sept. 23, '64
Wisner, J, 100, Sept. 24, '64
Wilson, G. M, Sept. 24, '64
Walker, G, 4, Sept. 27, '64
Wentley, J, 155, Sept. 28, '64
Wattson, W, 99, Sept. 30, '64
Weeks, C, 76, Oct. 2, '64
Waltz, J, 7, Oct. 2, '64
Weelkly, J, 14, Oct. 2, '64
Weeks, C, 76, Oct. 3, '64
Wolfhope, J, 184, Oct. 4, '64
Wilson, G, 55, Oct. 6, '64
Wilson, J, 118, Oct. 6, '64
Williams, W, 46, Oct. 8, '64
Walsh, W, 87, Oct. 9, '64
Welry, J. W, 116, Oct. 10, '64
Watts, A. J, 12, Oct. 11, '64
White, M, 21, Oct. 11, '64
Walker, W, 148, Oct. 12, '64
Wright, W, 16, Oct. 13, '64
Watson, C, 184, Oct. 15, '64
Wilderman, E, 14, Oct. 17, '64
Walker, A, 45, Oct. 17, '64
Welson, G, 140, Oct. 18, '64
Warrenton, J. H, 106, Oct. 26, '64
Walter, W, 184, Oct. 26, '64
Wood, J, 19, Oct. 26, '64
Woods, R. C, Art. Oct. 28, '64
Woodburn, J, 7, Nov. 1, '64
Weyncoop, F, 7, Nov. 2, '64
Weberter, J, 20, Nov. 7, '64
Wilkinson, C, 104, Nov. 12, '64
Weaver, J, 53, Nov. 13, '64
Walder, J, 5, Nov. 19, '64
Wider, H. N, 184, Nov. 19, '64
Weatherald, H. W, 7, Nov. 22, '64
Webb, C. M, 101, Nov. 23, '64
Wood, J. M, 2, Nov. 23, '64
Williamson, J, 145, Dec. 4, '64
Watson, H, 184, Jan. 2, '65
Williams, B, 95, Jan. 19, '65
Walker, H. G, 87, Jan. 20, '65
Wilkins, A, Art. Mar. 20, '65
Yocunib, W. B, 93, July 22, '64
Yocune, D, 1, Aug. 6, '64
Youst, W. A, 5, Aug. 7, '64
Yingling, E, 78, Aug. 18, '64
Yeager, S, 138, Aug. 22, '64
Young, J. B, 49, Oct. 2, '64
Young, W. H, 145, Oct. 17, '64
Yeager, A, 49, Nov. 6, '64
Zerphy, J, 79, June 10, '64
Zimmerman, B, 148, July 29, '64
Zane, W, 19, Aug. 23, '64
Zerb, J, 103, Aug. 25, '64
Zane, M, 118, Oct. 23, '64

www.ingramcontent.com/pod-product-compliance
Lightning Source LLC
Chambersburg PA
CBHW022008220426
43663CB00007B/1010